American English Primary Colors

Teacher's Book 2

Diana Hicks   Andrew Littlejohn

CAMBRIDGE UNIVERSITY PRESS

PUBLISHED BY THE PRESS SYNDICATE OF THE UNIVERSITY OF CAMBRIDGE
The Pitt Building, Trumpington Street, Cambridge, United Kingdom

CAMBRIDGE UNIVERSITY PRESS
The Edinburgh Building, Cambridge CB2 2RU, UK
40 West 20th Street, New York, NY 10011–4211, USA
477 Williamstown Road, Port Melbourne, VIC 3207, Australia
Ruiz de Alarcón 13, 28014 Madrid, Spain
Dock House, The Waterfront, Cape Town 8001, South Africa
43-45 Kreta Ayer Road, Singapore 089004
http://www.cambridge.org

© Cambridge University Press 2004

This book is in copyright. Subject to statutory exception
and to the provisions of relevant collective licensing agreements,
no reproduction of any part may take place without
the written permission of Cambridge University Press.

First published 2004

Printed in Singapore

Typeface Frutiger Roman. System QuarkXPress® [Pentacor]

ISBN 0 521 54849 7 Teacher's Book 2
ISBN 0 521 53920 X Student's Book 2
ISBN 0 521 53921 8 Activity Book 2
ISBN 0 521 53923 4 Class Audio CDs 2
ISBN 0 521 53922 6 Songs and Stories Audio CD 2
ISBN 0 521 60319 6 Vocabulary Cards 2

Contents

Map of the course	iv
Introduction	vi
The inside cover (Student's Book)	vii

Welcome!
A	My name's ...	4
B	King Cat's corner	6
C	Let's go!	8

Unit 1 Hello, Kip!
1A	Good dog!	10
1B	King Cat's corner	12
1C	Where's Kip?	14
1D	Storytime: Run!	16

Unit 2 Hello, Joanne!
2A	Where are we?	18
2B	King Cat's corner	20
2C	We're here!	22
2D	Storytime: The magic hat	24
Review		26

Unit 3 Hello, Zara!
3A	It's cold!	28
3B	King Cat's corner	30
3C	Help!	32
3D	Storytime: Eddie elephant	34

Unit 4 Hello, Tom!
4A	The birds	36
4B	King Cat's corner	38
4C	I can help.	40
4D	Storytime: Taffy the dog	42
Review		44

Unit 5 Hello, Ben!
5A	Sharks!	46
5B	King Cat's corner	48
5C	Thanks, Ben.	50
5D	Storytime: The smart fish	52

Unit 6 Goodbye!
6A	The tree	54
6B	King Cat's corner	56
6C	Come back, Kip!	58
6D	Storytime: The cages	60
Review		62

Word lists	64
A–Z: teaching young learners	65
Extra activities	
Games	79
Crafts	82
Extra practice	90
Tests	102
Templates	118
Acknowledgments	127

Map of the course

Welcome!

A My name's... 4–5	B King Cat's corner 6–7	C Let's go! 8–9
Hello. My name's... What's your name? **Possessives** my, your	It's a ... What is it? Is it a ...? Yes. No. a + noun My ...'s in my ... Oh, no. **Nouns** bag, classroom, notebook, pen, pencil, pencil case, marker, ruler	Goodbye. Let's ... What's that? It's a ... **Nouns** balloon, bus, car, cat, dog, house, park, school, sky, street, town **Verb** go **Adverb** up

1 Hello, Kip!

Plurals, Pronouns, be, numbers 1-10

1A Good dog! 10–11	1B King Cat's corner 12–13	1C Where's Kip? 14–15	1D STORYTIME Run! 16–17
What's in your ... ? **Plural nouns** They're very nice. They're my favorite. Where's my ... ? Here you are. Thanks. Stop. **Nouns** banana, cake, drink, lunchbox, sandwich, sweet, tummy **Adjectives** good, yummy	Numbers 1–10, point to the ... , stand up tall **Nouns** door, floor, wall, friend	What's this? It's a ... I don't know. Come on. **Nouns** book, farm, map	Lift off. **Nouns** planet, spaceship, markers, scissors, straw, tape **Verbs** open, run, see

2 Hello, Joanne!

Possessives, Pronouns, be, numbers 10-15

2A Where are we? 18–19	2B King Cat's corner 20–21	2C We're here! 22–23	2D STORYTIME The magic hat 24–25
Help. Hi. Welcome. Where's ...? She's here. He's there. **Nouns** place, teacher **Verbs** ask, clap, hop, jump **Pronouns** me, you **Adverbs** here, now	How old is (Steve)? He's (eight). What's his name? (Steve.) What's her name? (Nadia.) How old is he? He's (eight). How old is she? She's (six). How old are you? I'm (seven). (Six) and (seven) are ... We're here. Numbers 10–15 **Noun** birthday party **Possessive** his, her, our	This is my ... It's (big). Yes, it is. That's my ... No, it isn't. Where are we? **Nouns** children, desk, mouse, number **Adjective** big **Verb** look at	Wow. I like ... Where are you? (Karen) isn't (here). **Nouns** hat, paper **Adjective** magic

REVIEW (Welcome!, Units 1 & 2) 26–27

3 Hello, Zara!

Be negative, there is/there are, Adjectives

3A It's cold! 28–29	3B King Cat's corner 30–31	3C Help! 32–33	3D STORYTIME Eddie Elephant 34–35
Are you (cold)? Yes, I am. I'm very (cold). I'm not. Are they (dangerous)? Yes, they are. Is (Daniel / Maria) in a (balloon)? Yes, he is. / No, she isn't. **Nouns** bear, snow, ball **Verb** kick **Adjectives** cold, dangerous, small **Adverbs** down, round **Preposition** in	The (dog) is (green). (Blue)'s our favorite color. Are they (big)? Yes, they are. No, they aren't. **Adjectives** black, blue, brown, green, red, white, yellow	There's a ... There are ... They aren't ... I know. **Nouns** boy, girl, bear, garden, skis, tree **Verbs** yell, come **Adjective** strong **Preposition** on	Can you (help me)? Of course. **Nouns** elephant, man, glue, trunk **Adjective** hot

iv

4 Hello, Tom!

Can/can't, numbers 15-20

4A The birds 36–37
I can ... What can we do?
We can ...
Nouns bird, cow, horse
Verbs climb, count to, fly, go away, hear, read, write

4B King Cat's corner 38–39
Numbers 15–20
Noun dinner time
Pronoun everything
Adverb away

4C I can help. 40–41
I can't ... (A horse) can / can't ...
Nouns chick, duck, hen, leg(s), Dad, Mom
Verb walk
Adjective silly
Adverbs fast, high

4D STORYTIME
Taffy the dog 42–43
Stop it. We can't ...
You can ... Get out.
Go away. Thank you.
Nouns rain, telephone, umbrella, posterboard, mask, string
Verbs drive, go out, stay
Adjective smart

REVIEW (Units 3 & 4) 44–45

5 Hello, Ben!

Have, Present simple

5A Sharks! 46–47
We have ... I have ...
I think ... Let's see.
You have ...
Don't worry. They can ...
Nouns fish, island, sea, shark, ship, telescope
Verb eat
Adjective safe

5B King Cat's corner 48–49
He has ... She has ...
Nouns ear, eye(s), hair, head, mouth, nose
Verbs close, pull, say, pat
Adjectives blond, long, short

5C Thanks, Ben. 50–51
(Sharks) eat (people).
They eat ...
Who are you? We live ...
I know what that is.
I (see it) every day.
They live ...
Present simple:
in rivers, in forests, in the sea, on farms
Nouns animal, crocodile, monkey, tiger, boat, fruit, grass, people, tree house
Adjectives right, wrong
Adverb too

5D STORYTIME
The smart fish 52–53
You can't ... Yes, I can.
No, you can't.
Where is he?
Who's that?
Noun brother
Verb catch

6 Goodbye!

Present simple, questions, short answers

6A The tree 54–55
Do you like ...? Yes, I do.
No, I don't. Follow me.
Here we are. Why is it ... ?
Are you OK? I'm OK.
Let me think. I like it.
I like them.
Nouns apple, cheese, coconut, ice cream, milk, orange, pear
Verb do

6B King Cat's corner 56–57
What's next? Days of the week, go to school, go home, after school, do my homework, play soccer, watch TV, by bus, by car, by bike, on foot, go swimming, go to my music lesson, go to my friend's house, sleep

6C Come back, Kip! 58–59
Come and see. Wait a minute. Welcome back.
What can (Kip see / they do)?
Nouns cave, thing
Adjectives fantastic, new
Pronoun something

6D STORYTIME
The cages 60–61
I can't find ... I can help you. Tell us. You want to ... (My friends) want to ... He's right. We all want ...
Nouns cage, parrot, paper clip
Adjectives excellent, free, terrible

REVIEW (Units 5 & 6) 62–63

v

Introduction

American English Primary Colors is a course in English for children of elementary school age, who may be learning English in school or in a language institute. The course includes a level for complete beginners who have not yet learned to read or write (Level 1). This level, *American English Primary Colors 2*, is for children who have basic abilities in reading and writing in their mother tongue and who are familiar with the English alphabet. It can be used after *Level 1*, or with children who are complete beginners in English.

Each level of the course has these components:

- Student's Book
- Activity Book
- Teacher's Book
- Class CD
- Songs and Stories CD
- Vocabulary Cards

Student's Book

In *American English Primary Colors 2*, the Student's Book contains the following work for classroom use:

- a *Welcome!* unit with three sections.
- six further units, each with four sections. Sections A and C have a continuing story about some children on an adventure in a hot air balloon, followed by exercises and songs. Section B contains exercises and a chant, presented by "King Cat." Section D is called *Storytime*. It includes a self-contained story and a related craft activity.
- three *Review* sections.

Activity Book

The Activity Book is in full color. It contains:

- practice exercises for each unit, which the children can usually do either in the class or at home.
- a *Review* section at the end of every unit.
- a *Picture Dictionary* page for every unit.
- stickers which are to be used in a number of the exercises in the Activity Book.

Teacher's Book

This Teacher's Book contains:

- a map of the course.
- teaching notes, which are interleaved with the pages of the Student's Book. They provide guidance on each exercise, extra ideas, answers, tapescripts, and suggestions for instructional language that you can use.
- the *A–Z: teaching young learners* with many more ideas on important aspects of teaching children.
- photocopiable templates of cut-outs for the craft activities in the Student's Book and Activity Book.
- an *Extra activities* section with additional games and crafts.
- an *Extra practice* section for each unit, concentrating on reading and writing.
- tests for all units.

Teaching young learners

Teaching very young learners can be an extremely rewarding experience. They tend to be very eager and motivated, and have a readiness to learn that can make teaching a joy. However, it can also be very demanding. The following are some key points that experienced teachers have found important in successful teaching. You will find a lot of further support in the teaching notes, and more guidance and ideas in *A–Z: teaching young learners*. Further ideas and support materials for teaching children can be found at Andrew Littlejohn's website: www.AndrewLittlejohn.net

Patience

Young children generally take a long time to do things. A simple matter such as opening their book and writing the date can be an epic achievement. It may involve dropping pencils, losing sharpeners, writing on the wrong page, elbowing the person next to them, and so on! This is simply the nature of children, who are learning what it is to be in school. To deal with this, you have to be patient and help them to see how they can focus and organize themselves better. Experienced teachers emphasize the importance of talking calmly to the children about what they will be doing and why.

Introduction

Use English – but be flexible

Young children need a sense of security, and may become nervous and withdrawn if they feel that they cannot express themselves. We believe it is appropriate to use the mother tongue to create trust and rapport. At the same time, it is important to make sure that English becomes the "natural" language of the classroom. Use English as much as possible, with gestures and quick translations to be sure that everyone is following and has the same chance to learn.

Activity

Probably most people learn best by doing, but young children in particular need to be actively involved. Ask yourself continually *How can I involve them more? How can I bring about* their *activity (not mine)?* Activity that involves moving, making, and doing – using their whole personalities – is most important. Extensive grammar teaching is unlikely to work, as it will probably go in one ear and out the other.

Personal involvement

Activity is important, but it is equally important that the children are *personally* involved. This means that it is necessary to provide space and time for the children to contribute their ideas and experiences and to make decisions about what they will be doing. Create a sense of belonging in the class by sharing decisions, making the classroom *theirs*, displaying their work, and encouraging them to bring things in.

Opportunities to learn

A child who is not learning anything is usually a bored child. A bored child will eventually mentally "drop out" of the class, and may become disruptive. He or she may be a very capable child who feels the class is too easy, or a less capable one who feels lost. Use every opportunity to make the classroom rich with learning opportunities *for everyone* – opportunities not only to learn English, but also to learn about the world.

Encouragement

Children monitor the feedback that they and others get from you, the teacher. They always make comparisons and usually have a good idea of who the teacher thinks is the "best" in the class. It is usually best to avoid giving negative feedback, which can have a bad effect on motivation and damage the child's self-esteem. A more useful approach may be to phrase things positively: *That's a very good try. Well done. Let's see how you can make it even better.* Above all, it is important to believe that everyone can learn and to encourage the children to believe that too.

The way they see things

Sometimes we may jump to conclusions about why children do certain things but it is important to try to see the class through *their* eyes. For example, there may be one or two children who seem disinterested, and it is easy to conclude that "they just don't want to learn." However, the reality may be different. Most of us enjoy the things that we are good at and look forward to doing them again. Conversely, we don't like doing the things that we do badly and will avoid doing them if we can. The bored or resistant child may simply be trying to *avoid failing*. If you see things in this way, through the child's eyes, you can often recognize misbehavior or apparent lack of interest as a cry for extra help.

The final page: teaching notes

The final page of the Student's Book includes three sections that you can use when you like. It is *not* intended that you start the course with these sections. It is best to wait until the end of Unit 1, so that the children are familiar with the book.

Useful words

These are words that come up in exercise instructions. Read the words aloud slowly and clearly, and mime an action for each one. Encourage the children to do the actions with you. You could then play "Simon says" (see page T81 in this Teacher's Book).

The alphabet

To teach or review the alphabet in English, say three or four letters at a time and get the children to repeat. Then play the recording and get them to sing along. Rather than spending a lot of time all at once on the alphabet, it is better to return to it now and then, asking the children to spell some of the names and new words that they learn.

Alphabet song

This song practices the letters of the alphabet. Read the words with the children, checking that they know how to say the letters. Then play the song and get the children to sing. You can do this two or three times, adding new words each time. For example, they could spell *English* or the words from the "Useful words" section.

Welcome!

A My name's ...

1 🔊 Listen and follow.

A • My name's …

Topic
The children meet the main characters of the course: Jess, Nick, Kip, and King Cat. Jess and Nick are building a balloon which will take them on their adventures.

Aim
- To teach the children how to ask someone's name and introduce themselves.

Language
Hello!
My name's …
What's your name?

What you need
- CD and player
- Copies of Cut-out 1 (page T118 in the Teacher's Book) for Activity Book Exercise 3.
- Markers, card, scissors, and glue for Activity Book Exercise 3.

Using the mother tongue: Different teachers or schools have different policies on the use of the mother tongue in the classroom. While in general we recommend some use of the mother tongue (see **A–Z English and the mother tongue**), we have provided some alternative suggestions, where appropriate, for teachers who do not wish to use it.

Times: The times suggested for exercises are approximate indications only.

Before you begin
Before you begin, it is a good idea to give the children an opportunity to get to know the Student's Book. Some ideas (using the mother tongue):

- Allow the children to look through the book. Ask them to find their favorite picture.
- Ask them to find particular things, for example, a picture of a shark, pages where King Cat appears, something they can make, and so on.
- Ask them to find some information about the book, for example, how many pages it has, how many units it has, who wrote it, and so on.

STUDENT'S BOOK

  Listen and follow. 15 minutes

You could use one of these approaches:

- *With the mother tongue:* With books closed, play the recording through, and then play it again in sections. After each section (which corresponds to a picture in the Student's Book), pause the recording and ask the children what they think is happening. You can ask some questions: *What is the person doing? What is that screeching sound? What is that muffled sound?* The children can use their imagination and the recorded sound effects to guess.
- Alternatively, before you play the recording, look at the pictures with the children. Ask what they can see. What do they think Nick and Jess are doing? And what is Kip doing?
- *Without the mother tongue:* Introduce yourself to the class with *Hello! My name's …* Say this once or twice, and then ask *What's your name?* Help one or two children to say their name with the expression *My name's …* Exercise 2 practices this further, so at this point it is only an introduction.

LISTENING TO THE STORY Play the recording. Point at the character who is speaking in each picture as the recording plays. Play it again, and this time get the children to point at the characters.

Point at the characters again and ask the name of each one. Alternatively, hold up Vocabulary Cards 3, 4, and 5.

Classroom language and answer key

Hello! My name's …
What's your name?

Listen.
Follow.
Look.

What's his name?
What's her name?

A • My name's …

This is King Cat.
Listen.

My name's …
What's your name?

2 🔊 Listen and answer. Ask your friend. [10 minutes]

Ask the children to look at the pictures of King Cat. Then play the recording.

Ask a child *What's your name?* Repeat this a few times with different children. Get one or two children to ask others.

If possible, use the children's mother tongue to introduce the idea of group work. Explain to them what they are going to do and that work in pairs or groups will help them get more practice so that they can learn faster. Then move them into groups (four children in each group is ideal).

The children take turns to introduce themselves to each of the others in the group and ask their names. As they work, go around and listen.

Further practice: Activity Book Exercises 2 and 3.

3 🔊 Sing a song. [10 minutes]

Play the recording once or twice and encourage the children to sing. They can follow you and mime actions: wave for *Hello, hello!*, point for *What's your name?*, and point at themselves for *My name's …*

Listen.
Sing a song.

Get the class to sing without the recording. Point at one child after they have sung *What's your name?* That child then sings his/her name and the class sings *Hello, (name)!* Continue around the class with a few more children. If individuals feel shy, it is best not to push them. Simply say their name for them, and carry on.

ACTIVITY BOOK

Note: If the children use the Activity Book at home, it is important to look at the exercises with them in class beforehand.

1 Use the stickers (page St.1). [10 minutes]

Choose the sticker.
Stick the stickers in the picture.

Get the class to find the stickers in the middle of the Activity Book. Check that they know which stickers they need for this exercise by asking them to point to the ones they are going to use. The children decide which stickers go where, and stick them to the pictures.

2 Draw your picture. Write your name. [10 minutes]

The children now draw a picture of themselves. They can add a speech bubble and write *Hello! My name's (name).* Instead of drawing their picture in the Activity Book, they could draw it on a separate piece of paper. You could then make an attractive display to put on the wall.

3 Make a bookmark. [10 minutes]

Optional: use Cut-out 1, page T118 in the Teacher's Book.

Draw a balloon.
Cut here.
Color the balloon.
Write your name.

To make the balloon bookmark, the children need a small piece of posterboard the size of a postcard (or bigger). You can make photocopies of the cut-out on page T118 of the Teacher's Book. The children stick it onto the posterboard and carefully cut it out. Alternatively, you can show them how to draw and cut out their own balloon, following the instructions in the Activity Book.

EXTRA IDEA There are more bookmark ideas in *Extra activities*, page T83 in the Teacher's Book.

2 🔊 Listen and answer. Ask your friend.

3 🔊 Sing a song.

Hello, hello, hello!
What's your name?
What's your name?

Hello, hello, hello!
My name's Jess.
My name's Jess.

Hello, Jess!

B King Cat's corner

1 Say the words.

It's ...

a notebook   a marker   a ruler   a pencil   a pencil case   a pen

2 Find the things. Say the words.   A ruler.

6

B • King Cat's corner

Topic
The children meet King Cat again. He teaches them some new words, and in the Activity Book he has some puzzles for them to do.

Aim
- To teach the names of some common classroom objects.
- To teach the use of *It's a ...* and *Is it a ...?*

Language
It's a ...
What is it?
Is it a ...?
Yes. No.
My pen's in my bag.
Where's my pen?
notebook, marker, pencil, ruler, pencil case, pen, bag, classroom

What you need
- CD and player.
- Classroom objects for Exercise 1: ruler, pen, marker, notebook, pencil, pencil case, book.
- Optional: small pieces of paper (six per child) for Exercise 1.
- Bags or large envelopes for Exercise 3.

Before you begin
You could begin by singing the song from Section A again.

STUDENT'S BOOK

  Say the words.   12 minutes

To teach the names of the objects, hold up an example of each thing, or use Vocabulary Cards 7–12. Get the children to say the names after you. Repeat this a few times.

Play the recording. The children point at the picture for each word in their books.

To practice the words, there are a number of interesting things you could choose:
- Mime an action associated with each word ("writing" with a pen/pencil/marker, "measuring" with a ruler, "reading" a book, etc.). The children guess the objects. Some children could also mime for the class.
- Ask the children to cover the words in the book with small pieces of paper. In pairs, one child points to a picture and the other says the name.
- Put an object in a bag and bring it out very slowly. The children have to guess what the object is.
- Play "Kim's game" (see *Extra activities*, page T81 in the Teacher's Book).

2 Find the things. Say the words.   10 minutes

The children look at the picture and try to find the objects from Exercise 1. Give them a few minutes to find them, and then ask them to show you where they are. They can point at objects in the picture and name them. (There are four notebooks, one marker, and two of each of the other objects in the picture.) **Further practice:** Activity Book Exercises 1 and 2.

Classroom language and answer key

Listen.
Say the name.
What's the word?
What is it?

Look at the picture.
Find the things.
Where is it?
Look. A ruler.

B • King Cat's corner

Let's play a game.

Listen.
Say the sentence.
All together.

Answers
1 What's 2 pen 3 ruler
4 pencil 5 book 6 name's
7 marker

Answers
marker, notebook

Choose the sticker.
Stick the stickers on the picture.

Let's play a game.
Draw four things.
It's a secret!
Guess!
Say a word.

3 Play a game. 12 minutes

Look at the pictures with the children and read the speech bubbles aloud so they get the idea of this guessing game. Before they play in pairs, you can play the game with a few children in front of the class.

Hand a bag to each pair. The children take turns to secretly put an object in the bag for their partner to guess. If you don't have bags available, pairs can put their objects in a large envelope, between the pages of a book, or under a cloth or item of clothing.

4 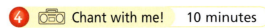 **Chant with me!** 10 minutes

First, play the recording all the way through. Then play it again sentence by sentence, and encourage the children to say it with the rhythm. It is a good idea to hold up the appropriate objects as they say them in the chant.

EXTRA IDEAS
- Hold up some other objects (e.g. a marker) as prompts for new verses.
- Divide the class in half. One half says the first two sentences, and the other half says the next two.
- Change the words to names of people. In this case, ask some children to come to the front of the classroom. Point at one of them, and get the class to chant *(Name)'s in my classroom* (twice). That child then runs away and the class chants *Oh no! Oh no! Where's (name)?* Point at another child and continue in the same way. If they all run to the same place, you can point at them at the end and they can chant *Here!*

Further practice: Activity Book Exercises 3 and 4.

ACTIVITY BOOK

1 Write the words. 10 minutes

You may need to explain to the children how these word puzzles work. You could make one up and do it on the board as an example.

2 Color the dots. Draw the pictures. 15 minutes

The children first color in the shapes with dots in them – this will spell a word. They then draw the object in the space below.

3 Use the stickers (page St.1). 5 minutes

New language: book

The children will find the stickers in the middle of the Activity Book. Remind them that they have to complete the pictures with the correct stickers. Check that they know which stickers they need for the exercise by asking them to point to the ones they are going to use. The children decide which stickers go where, and stick them to the pictures.

4 Play a game. 20 minutes

Note: This exercise is intended for classroom use.

Divide the class into pairs. Each child secretly draws three objects on a piece of paper. (You can put a list of objects on the board.) In their pairs, they take turns guessing an object that their partner has drawn. The first person to guess all three objects is the winner.

3 Play a game.

4 🔊 Chant with me!

My pen's in my bag.
My pen's in my bag.

Oh, no! Oh, no!
Where's my pen?

My ruler's in my bag.
My ruler's in my bag.

My bag's in my classroom.
My bag's in my classroom.

Let's go!

1 Listen and follow.

C • Let's go!

Topic
Jess, Nick, and Kip take off in the balloon. They fly over a town and see different things on the ground.

Aim
- To teach the names of objects in a town.
- To teach the use of *What's that?* and practice *It's a ...*

Language
Goodbye!
Up in a balloon.
What's that?
It's a ...
town, car, dog, street, bus, park, school, in the sky

What you need
- CD and player.
- Optional: cardboard rolls, a large box, and pictures of town objects for Exercise 1.
- Copies of Cut-out 2 (Teacher's Book, page T119) and scissors for Exercise 3.
- Copies of Cut-out 3 (Teacher's Book, page T119) for Activity Book Exercise 2.
- Posterboard, scissors, glue, and pencils for Activity Book Exercise 2.

Before you begin

- *With the mother tongue:* Before they open their books, ask the children to imagine that they are in a hot air balloon over their town. What can they see? On the board, write the English words for some of the things they mention.
- *Without the mother tongue:* Draw a simple picture of a hot air balloon on the board. Say *Look! A balloon.* Draw the outline of a town beneath it: a house, a school, a street, a car, a bus. Ask *What's that?* Then give an answer and write *It's a ...* and the name of each object.

STUDENT'S BOOK

 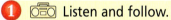

Classroom language and answer key

Look at the pictures with the children. Say *Look! A balloon.* Then turn back to page 4, and point to the pictures to show that it's the same balloon.

Turn back to page 8 and ask them what they can see. Point at the different things in the picture of the town and say the names. For the moment, the children can just listen and follow you.

What's that?
It's a ...

LISTENING TO THE STORY Play the recording. Ask the children to point at the words as they listen. (This is not an easy thing to do for many children of this age, as it requires using abilities simultaneously. Don't be surprised if they can't do it to begin with.) Play the recording two or three times.

Listen and point.

Get the children to tell you the new words by holding up Vocabulary Cards 14–21 (or by pointing at the objects in the picture) and asking *What's that?*

What's that?

Read the dialog aloud. You could take the part of Jess and get different children to take the part of Nick. Make sure they pronounce the *s* correctly in *What's* and *It's*. When you reach Kip's question at the end of the dialog, ask the class to answer it *(It's a cat.)*.

ACTING OUT Divide the class into pairs and get them to read the dialog.

Work in pairs.
Say the conversation.

You could then ask some children to act out the story for the class. Ask for volunteers and choose two or three pairs. Acting out can be a lot more memorable and fun if you provide some props. For example:

- "binoculars" made from cardboard rolls.
- pictures of a cat, a dog, a school, etc. which the children can point at.
- a box to stand in, simulating the balloon basket.

Who wants to act out the story?
Very good!
Well done!

Further practice: Activity Book Exercise 1.

C • Let's go!

Listen and sing!
Let's sing it again.
And now you.

Cut out the binoculars.

Put it over the picture.
What's that?
It's a …

Answers
2 It's a bus. 3 It's a school.
4 It's a park. 5 It's a balloon.
6 It's a house. 7 It's a town.

Let's make spinners.
Cut out the spinner.
Paste it on the card.
Color it.
Put the pencil in the middle.

2 Sing a song.   10 minutes

Play the song and encourage the children to sing. Use gesture to show the meaning of *in the sky*.

EXTRA IDEAS
- Divide the class into halves, with one half asking the question in the second verse and the other half answering it.
- Add other words to the song by holding up classroom objects from Section B (pen, pencil, notebook, etc.).

3 Think. Play a game.   10 minutes

You will need copies of Cut-out 2 (page T119 in the Teacher's Book).

Hand out copies of Cut-out 2 and get the children to cut out the binoculars and the lens holes. Alternatively, depending on the abilities of your class, you might want to have them cut beforehand.

Divide the class into pairs. Explain to the children that they have to cover an object in the picture with the binoculars and only slowly reveal it to their partner. Demonstrate once or twice in front of the class. Then get the children to do it themselves in pairs. Go around the room and listen to what they say.

EXTRA IDEAS
- You or the children could glue the binoculars onto card and then cut the lens holes. This way, they will last longer.
- Collect the binoculars so that the children can use them again later. They can play the binoculars game with any of the large pictures in the book.

Further practice: Activity Book Exercise 2.

ACTIVITY BOOK

Note: The spinners are an important element in the course.
The children will need them frequently. Make sure they are kept safe.

1 Write the words.   10 minutes

The children have to look carefully at the pictures and decide what they are. They then write a complete sentence, following the example.

2 Make a spinner. Play a game. Color the board.   20+ minutes

Note: This exercise needs to be done in the classroom.
Use Cut-out 3 (Teacher's Book, page T119).

The spinner is used in Section C of every unit in the Activity Book, and also in the games in *Review* sections in the Student's Book after Units 2, 4, and 6. Here, the children make their spinner before they play the game.

Make the spinner: Hand out photocopies of Cut-out 3 which the children can then color, glue on posterboard, and cut out. They then put a pencil through the middle so that it can spin and land on different numbers.

Play the game: The children can play the game in pairs or threes. One of them spins the spinner. If it lands, for example, on number 3, one of the other children points to picture 3 and asks *What's that?* The first child has to say what it is. Note that the game is printed in black and white so that the children can color it in either before or after playing.

2 🎵 Sing a song.

Up, up, up,
Up in a balloon.
Up, up, up,
Up in the sky!

It's a cat!

What's that?
What's that?
It's a cat!
It's a cat!

It's a car!

It's a park!

3 Think. Play a game.

You need:
cut-out 2

a school

a cat

Act it out!

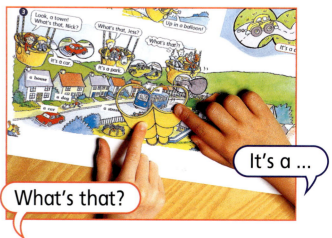

What's that?

It's a ...

9

1 Hello, Kip!

1A Good dog!

1  Listen and follow.

Act it out!

1A • Good dog!

Topic
Jess and Nick are back on the ground. They are comparing what they have in their lunchboxes but Kip runs off with Nick's lunchbox.

Aims
- To teach the regular plural form.
- To teach the names of some foods.

Language
Good dog!
What's in your lunchbox?
Bananas are nice.
They're very nice.
They're my favorite.
Here you are. Thanks.
sandwich, drink, cupcake, banana, sweet, tummy, yummy

What you need
- CD and player.
- Optional: a lunchbox containing fruit, cupcake, etc. for Exercise 1.

Before you begin
- *With the mother tongue:* Ask what the children remember about Jess, Nick, and Kip.
- *Without the mother tongue:* On the board, draw a simple picture of a balloon with two people and a dog in the basket. Ask *What's his/her name?* Then draw some town objects from *Welcome!* C under the balloon and see if the children can remember the words.

STUDENT'S BOOK

1 **Listen and follow.** 20+ minutes

To prepare for the activity, you could bring a lunchbox into the class and show the children what food you have in it. Tell them what your favorite thing is.

If the children bring lunchboxes to school, you could look through some with them. Say the names of some of the things you find and comment on them. Try to use the plural form, as this is a key point of this section. For example: *Mmmm. Apples. Apples are my favorite.*

LISTENING TO THE STORY Allow the children to look at the pictures for a minute or two. Ask *What's in Jess's lunchbox?* and repeat the question in the mother tongue if possible. Draw a picture for each item on the board, or hold up Vocabulary Cards 22–26. Say the question and then the answer while you point at each item. Ask the question again, and encourage the children to answer.

Play the recording through a few times. Take Jess's part and get different children to take the parts of Nick and Kip.

Draw attention to the plural form. You can draw (for example) a banana on the board and say *Look. A banana.* Add another one and say *Look. Two bananas.* Continue in a similar way with the objects they learned in the *Welcome!* unit (*pen, ruler, book,* etc.) and different numbers (*three pens, five rulers,* etc.).

EXTRA IDEA You could ask some children to act out the story.

Classroom language and answer key

Look at my lunchbox.
... are my favorite.
They're nice.
What's in your lunchbox?

Look at the pictures.
What's in Jess's lunchbox?
You can answer.

Listen.
You are Nick/Kip.

1A • Good dog!

What can you see?
Close your books.
Listen. Listen again.
Draw a line.

Answers
Jess: two cupcakes, a sandwich, a drink, two bananas.
King Cat: A drink, a sandwich, two cupcakes.
Nick: A sweet, a drink, a sandwich, two bananas, two cupcakes.

2 Listen and match. Ask your friend. 10 minutes

You could teach the word *sweet* with the help of Vocabulary Card 27. Then look at the pictures with the children and get them to tell you what each thing is.

Ask them to close their books and play the recording. Pause after each character has spoken and ask what they have in their lunchbox.

The children can then open their books, listen again, and draw lines to the objects. If you don't want them to write in their books, they can write or draw the objects under the names *Nick*, *Jess*, and *King Cat* in their notebooks.

Tapescript
Narrator: Hello, Jess. What's in your lunchbox?
Jess: Hello. Er ... Let's see. Two cupcakes, a sandwich, a drink, and two bananas. Mmmmmm. Yummy, yummy.
Narrator: Hello, King Cat. What's in your lunchbox?
King Cat: Mmmm. Let's see. A drink, a sandwich, and ... two cupcakes!
Narrator: Nick, what's in your lunchbox?
Nick: My lunchbox! A sweet, a drink, a sandwich, two bananas, and two cupcakes. But where's my lunchbox? Kip! Kip! Kip!

Further practice: Activity Book Exercises 1 and 2.

3 Sing a song. 10 minutes

You can mime to this song. The children can mime with you for each object – for example, peeling a banana, biting a cupcake, unwrapping a sweet. They can rub their stomach for *Yummy, yummy*, and pat it for the last line.
Further practice: Activity Book Exercises 3 and 4.

ACTIVITY BOOK

1 Use the stickers (page St.1). 20 minutes

Help the children to find the stickers in the middle of the Activity Book and elicit the names for these food items. Make certain that the children know which stickers they need by asking them to point to the ones they are going to use. They decide which sticker goes where, and stick them to the pictures.

Listen and sing.
Let's sing it again.
Do the actions.

2 Write the words. 5 minutes

Before the children write in their answers, go through them first. Point out that there is only one of each thing, so they do not add *s*.

What's this?
Choose the sticker.
Stick the stickers on the picture.

3 Write and say. 5 minutes

New language: fruit, apples, pears, oranges, milk, cola, water, juice, TV program.

The meaning of the new words should be clear from the pictures, but you may want to read them aloud to establish the correct pronunciation. For *... is my favorite sweet*, the children can write the name of a local sweet.

Answers
2 cake 3 drink 4 sandwich
5 pen 6 car

4 Draw lines. 5 minutes

The children have to read through the sentences and decide which goes where.

Answers
1 Here you are. Thanks.
2 Where's my pen?
3 What's in your lunchbox?

2 🔊 Listen and match. Ask your friend.

3 🔊 Sing a song.

Bananas, Bananas!

They're very nice.
They're my favorite.

Yummy, yummy, yummy,
In my tummy, tummy, tummy!

Cakes   Sweets

Oh, my tummy!

1B King Cat's corner

1 Listen, say, and write the numbers.

1	2	3		
one	two	three	four	five
six	seven	eight	nine	ten

2 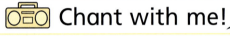 Chant with me!

1, 2, 3, point to the door!

3, 4, 5, point to the floor!

5, 6, 7, point to the wall!

8, 9, 10, stand up tall!

1B • King Cat's corner

Topic
King Cat has some number puzzles for the children to do.

Aims
- To teach the numbers 1–10.
- To review and practice the plural form.

Language
Numbers 1–10
Point to …
Stand up tall.
door, floor, wall

What you need
- CD and player.

Before you begin

This section teaches the numbers 1-10. It is probably best to teach them in two blocks: 1-5 and then 5-10. You can use pens or other classroom objects and say the number as you hold them up. The children then repeat after you. Many children may already know some numbers, so you will have to judge how much time you need to spend on this.

STUDENT'S BOOK

 1 Listen, say, and write the numbers. **10 minutes**

Play the recording once and get the children to say the numbers. Then play it again, pause at each number, and get them to say the next one – the recording will then confirm whether or not they are correct.

The children then write the correct number over each word. Alternatively, they can copy the numbers into their notebooks and write the words under each one.

EXTRA IDEAS

- Say numbers at random from 1-10 and ask the children to say the next number.
- Write the numbers 1-10 on the board, close your eyes, and randomly point at one of them. The children have to say the number.
- Use the numbers to play "Bingo" or "The number game" (see *Extra activities*, pages T80 and T81 in the Teacher's Book).
- Play a "Find" game. Write five or six numbers on the board. In pairs, the children have to find items in the classroom or in the book that match each number, for example, five rulers.

 2 Chant with me! **10 minutes**

This is an action chant. Before you play the recording, read the words to the children and get them to do the actions. In the final line, they should stand up. Encourage them to say the words with you.

Then play the recording. The children do the actions and say the words at the same time.

EXTRA IDEA Divide the class into two or four groups. They take turns saying the lines of the chant while everybody does the actions.

Classroom language and answer key

Listen.
Say it after me.
What's the next number?

Look at the numbers.
Count and write the number.

Let's do a chant.
Watch me!
Do the actions.

1B • King Cat's corner

What's the next number?

Answers
One, two, three, four, five.
Two, four, six, eight, ten.
One, three, five, seven, nine.

3 Think. Say the next two numbers. 5 minutes

Read the speech bubbles to the children and ask them what they think the next numbers are. Then play the recording and get them to say the next numbers.

EXTRA IDEAS
- You can teach a few more numbers (*eleven* and *twelve*) and then write some sequences on the board for the children to complete. For example:
  one, four, seven, ...   three, six, nine ....   ten, eight, ..., four
- The children could write some sequences for their neighbor to complete.

Further practice: Activity Book Exercises 2 and 3.

4 Play a game. Draw and say. 20+ minutes

This pair work game provides extra practice with the plural form. Ideally, pairs should sit back to back. If this is not possible, they must keep their drawing hidden from their partner. If they are not allowed to draw in their books, ask them to copy the pictures of the bags into their notebooks.

In the bag labeled *Your bag*, each child draws four or five collections of objects, for example, three cupcakes, five pencils. They then tell their partner, who draws the objects in the bag labeled *Your friend's bag*. Go around the class and listen. Make sure that they are saying the final *s* correctly for the plural form.

When they have finished, they can check if they are correct by looking at their partner's picture.

Further practice: Activity Book Exercise 1.

ACTIVITY BOOK

Turn your chairs around.
Hide your book.
Don't look!
Tell your neighbor.

Answers
Picture A: 5 notebooks, 3 pencils, 3 bags, 2 cats, 2 drinks, 5 cars
Picture B: 6 notebooks, 4 pencils, 4 bags, 1 cat, 3 drinks, 1 car

1 Think. Find six more differences. 10+ minutes

Ask the children to write lists of differences in their notebooks. If you do the exercise in the classroom, they can work in pairs to find the seven differences, and you can go through the answers with the class. You can use *he/she has* when you are talking about the pictures, but this is not a teaching point here. Don't expect the children to use this form, but make sure that they say the plural form correctly.

2 Think. Write the words. 5 minutes

Explain to the children that they have to write the missing numbers in words. They can read the sums across or down.

You could give them another puzzle to do, for example:

(?)	+	two	=	nine	(seven)
–		+		–	
three	–	(?)	=	one	(two)
=		=		=	
four	+	four	=	(?)	(eight)

Answers
nine	–	seven	=	two
+		–		+
one	+	three	=	four
=		=		=
ten	–	four	=	six

Write four numbers.
Guess!
Say a number.
Say "yes" or "no."

3 Play a game. 5 minutes

Note: This exercise needs to be done in the classroom.

The children write numbers and try to guess what their partner has written. To help them, you can write the numbers 1–10 in words and digits on the board.

3 Think. Say the next two numbers.

4 Play a game. Draw and say.

Three bananas.

Your bag Your friend's bag

1C Where's Kip?

1 🔊 Listen and follow.

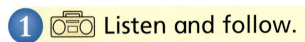

Act it out!

1C • Where's Kip?

Topic
Kip, who has taken Nick's lunchbox, finds a mysterious map with an X marked on it. Jess and Nick take off in the balloon to find out what the X is.

Aims
- To teach *What's this?*
- To review and practice numbers and plurals.

Language
Where's ...?
What's this?
It's a ...
I don't know.
Come on!
Let's go!
and, but
farm, book, map

What you need
- CD and player.
- Optional: five or six pens (or similar objects) to hide in the classroom for Exercise 3.
- The children will need their spinners for Activity Book Exercise 3.

Before you begin
You could start the lesson with the song from Unit 1A and the chant from Unit 1B. This will refresh the children's memory of plurals and the numbers 1–10.

STUDENT'S BOOK

1 **Listen and follow.** 20+ minutes

You could use one of these approaches:
- *With the mother tongue:* Before you play the recording, ask the children what is happening in the pictures.
- *Without the mother tongue:* Point at things in the picture, for example the lunchbox and the balloon, and ask *What's this?* Teach *a map* as you point at the map. You could also ask *Who's this?*, supplying and then eliciting the answers *It's Nick/Jess/Kip*.

LISTENING TO THE STORY Play the recording while the children follow the pictures in their books. Pause after picture 3 and ask *Where's Nick's lunchbox? Where's Kip?* The children point at the pictures. You can also point at the pictures and say *Yes, it's here!* or *Yes, he's here!*

Play the recording for pictures 4 and 5. Point to the map, then to the town, and the farm on the map, and ask *What's this?* Supply the answers. Then hold up Vocabulary Cards 14, 28, and 29, ask the same question and get individual children to answer.

Point at the X marking a spot on the map. Ask *What's this?* with a puzzled look on your face, and then supply the answer *I don't know*. Ask a few children, and elicit the same answer.

Play the recording for picture 6, and then play the whole dialog once or twice again.

ACTING OUT The children now say the dialog in pairs with their books open. Then ask them to close their books and try to say it again. Don't expect them to get it 100% correct: the important thing here is to build up their confidence as users of English. To help them remember, you can put six simple drawings on the board, one for each picture and each one with a question mark beside it. For example:

1 lunchbox   2 Kip   3 sandwich and drink   4 map   5 X   6 lunchbox

Some of the children can now act out the story for the class.

Classroom language and answer key

What's this?

Open your books.
Follow the story.
Listen.
Where's Kip? He's here!

What's this?
It's a ...

What's this?
I don't know ...

Close your books.
Say the conversation.
Look at the board.

Who wants to act out the story?
Very good! Well done!

1C • Where's Kip?

What's this?

Look at the pictures.
Choose a picture.
Ask your friend. Take turns.

Answers
1 It's a pen. 2 It's a ruler.
3 It's a book. 4 It's a pencil.
5 It's a banana. 6 It's a bag.

Look! A pen.
Let's count.
Two pens.

Look at the picture.
Count the pens/rulers (etc.).
Write the number.

Answers
8 pens, 10 rulers, 8 books,
9 pencils, 4 bags, 3 maps,
7 erasers 6 notebooks

Answers
2 It's a ruler. 3 It's a cupcake.
4 It's a map. 5 It's a door.
6 It's a car. 7 It's a bus.

Answers
house, dog, cat, pencil

2 Ask your friend. Think.   5 minutes

You could start with a game. Take a pencil and almost completely hide it in your hands. Show a very small part of it and ask the children *What's this?* Elicit *I don't know*. Gradually show more, until someone says *It's a pencil*. Do the same with a short ruler. You could secretly give an eraser or a pen to a child and get him/her to conceal it and go around the class, asking in the same way.

Now ask the children to look at the pictures. Point at the first one and ask *What's this?* Elicit answers. Then tell the children to ask each other in pairs. They should choose pictures at random and take turns.

EXTRA IDEA You can ask children to point at a picture and ask another child in another part of the classroom.

Further practice: Activity Book Exercises 1 and 2.

3 What's in the classroom? Look and count.   10 minutes

You could start with a game. Before the lesson, hide five or six pens in different parts of the classroom where they can be seen by the children if they look carefully. Point out one of the pens and say *Look! A pen*. Then "find" another pen and say *Let's count. One, two. Two pens*. Walk close to where another pen is and show that you are looking for it. The children can shout *Three! Four! Five!* as they see the other pens. You can elicit the whole phrase *Three pens* (etc.) as they discover each one.

Ask the children to look at the picture. Point to a pen in the picture. Say *Let's count. One, two …* and, with the children, count all the pens you can find. Then ask them to look for the other things with their neighbor. Tell them to look carefully, count, and write the number.

Go through their answers with them. You could ask *How many rulers/books (etc.)?* and ask a different pair to point and count for each object.

Further practice: Activity Book Exercise 3.

ACTIVITY BOOK

1 Match the parts. Write the words.   15 minutes

Go through the exercise orally with the children before they write their answers. They need to join the two halves of each picture together and then write the word in a complete sentence. If they are doing the exercise in class, you could put the answers on the board in random order to help those children who need extra support.

2 Color the dots. Write the words.   15 minutes

The children can use any color to shade in the dots and discover the words. If they do it in class, go through their answers orally before they write.

3 Play a game. Use your spinner. Color the board.   10 minutes

Note: This exercise has to be done in class. The children need their spinners.

The exercise reviews numbers and vocabulary in the form of a game, using the spinners that the children made in *Welcome!* C (see teaching notes on the Activity Book on page T9). When they spin their spinner and land on a number, they need to count the objects in the matching picture and say the number to their partner (*Seven sweets*, etc.). At the end, they can color in the pictures.

② Ask your friend. Think.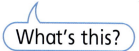

1
2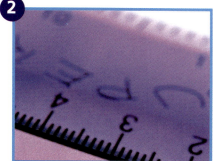
3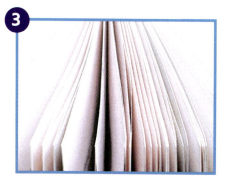
4
5
6

③ What's in the classroom? Look and count.

☐ pens
☐ rulers
☐ books
☐ pencils
☐ bags
☐ maps
☐ erasers
☐ notebooks

15

1D Run!

1. 🔊 Listen and follow.

1D • Storytime: Run!

Topic
Two astronauts go to a distant planet. They are terrified when they see an alien and make a quick return to Earth.

Aims
- To develop the children's listening and speaking fluency.
- To review numbers and *What's that?/ It's a ...*

Language
Review
Numbers 1–10
What's that?
It's a ...

New vocabulary
Lift off!
Let's see!
Open the door.
planet, run, spaceship

What you need
- CD and player.
- Optional: copies of Cut-out 4 (Teacher's Book, page T120) for Exercise 2.
- Drinking straws, markers, scissors, and tape for Exercise 2.
- Optional: a ready-made spaceship model for Exercise 2.
- Optional: clothes or a mask to dress up as an "alien" in Exercise 3.

*Note: Storytime sections come at the end of each unit. The stories are self-contained and separate from the balloon story with Nick, Jess, and Kip. They are intended to be enjoyed as stories although they also review language presented in the previous sections. Each story includes a craft activity. It is a good idea to make the model yourself before the lesson so that you can see how it works. The craft activities are an important element of the course. They make the English lessons more memorable and more tangible and create physical involvement with learning. They also provide a stimulus for the children's imagination. See **A–Z Stories**.*

Before you begin
Draw a simple picture of a rocket on the board. Ask the children what it is, and add pictures of the moon and other planets. You could change the order of the exercises and start by making the spaceship in Exercise 2. This will stimulate the children's interest in the story.

STUDENT'S BOOK

 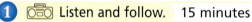

Classroom language and answer key

You could use one of these approaches:
- *With the mother tongue:* Ask the children to close their books. Play the recording all the way through. Then play it again in sections and ask them in their mother tongue what they think is happening.
- *Without the mother tongue:* You can ask the children to look at the pictures. Point to different things (the rocket, a town, a door, a house) and ask *What's that?* You could also teach **astronaut**.

What's that?
It's a ...

Play the recording while the children follow the story in their books.

Listen and follow.

Divide the class into pairs. Each child takes a part in the story, reading from the book. Alternatively, they could work in threes, with the extra person making the sound effects of the rocket and the door, and acting as the alien on the planet. Go around the class, listening to the pairs/groups.

Practice in pairs.
Read the story.

1D • Run!

Draw two rectangles.
Cut out the rectangles.
Color them in.

Make a ring.
Tape the ends together.

Stick the straw inside the ring.

Who wants to act out the story?
Use your spaceship.
Very good!
Well done!

Answers
trees: 4/four balloons: 6/six
flowers: 3/three birds: 8/eight
balls: 5/five ice cream: 7/seven
pen: 1/one cars: 9/nine
windows: 2/two dogs: 10/ten

Answers
```
x t d r i n k g g b
f w j h p t a r m a
b a n a n a a k q p
l u n c h b o x g w
f d b a g y a f p o
j h u e t f c v s k
g k a t w v m a p g
j n r t o w n j a g
j k m l p a s t w e
g f h e y s w e e t
```

Answers
1 b ten c nine d two e eight
  f seven g six h four
2 b nine erasers c eight pencils d seven bags
  e five drinks f ten books
  g six cupcakes h three rulers i four notebooks
3 It's a sandwich. It's a drink.
  What's that? It's a cupcake.
  What's this? It's a banana.
4 1 c 2 a 3 b 4 d

2 Make a spaceship.   20+ minutes

Optional: use Cut-out 4 (Teacher's Book, page T120).

This simple spaceship flies well if the instructions are followed precisely. It might be a good idea for you to make one in front of the children, so that they can see exactly what they have to do and how it flies.

You may want to prepare some of the materials beforehand, although, ideally, the more the children do for themselves, the better. Some questions to consider:
- Should the children draw their own strips or should you use photocopies of Cut-out 4? If they make their own, they will need to use rulers.
- Should you cut the paper into strips, or should they? If they do the cutting, make sure that they use children's scissors with rounded blades.
- Will you attach the straws to the inside of the paper rings, or will the children do it? This is the most complicated part of the model.

You will need to experiment to improve the flight of the rocket. If it drops quickly, move the rings apart. If it rises up at the front, move the rings closer together.

3 Act out the story. Use your spaceship.   10 minutes

You can now ask some children to act out the story, using their own spaceship. They can raise it as they make the sound effects for lift off, and move it through the air as they approach the planet. At the end, they can throw the rocket through the air. Whooooosh!

ACTIVITY BOOK Review

1 Draw lines.   10 minutes

New language: trees, balls, flowers, windows, ice cream cones, birds

The children need to match each picture with a figure and a number word. They have not yet learned the names for all of the objects shown, but these are not required to do the exercise. If you wish, however, you can teach these words now.

2 Find seven more things. Draw lines.   10 minutes

Check that the children know the name of each object before they look for the words in the puzzle.

I can …

The *I can …* sections help the children to see how much they have learned. Read through the three headings with the children and ask them for examples. They can then color in the stars.

Picture Dictionary 1

The children can now complete Picture Dictionary 1 on page 26. First, make sure they find the stickers in the middle of the Activity Book. Look at them together and check that they know where to stick them.

EXTRA PRACTICE There are optional *Extra practice* exercises for this unit on pages T90 and T91 in the Teacher's Book. This *Extra practice* section provides further review for teachers who wish to develop the children's accuracy in English and to give further practice in reading and writing.

What's that?
It's a planet.
Run!
Aaaaaah!

2 Make a spaceship.

You need: cut-out 4
scissors a straw tape markers

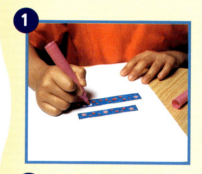
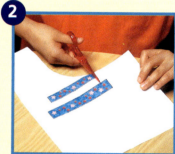

3 Act out the story.
Use your spaceship.

2 Hello, Joanne!

2A Where are we?

1 🔊 Listen and follow.

Act it out!

2A • Where are we?

Topic
Jess and Nick are up in their balloon, but the wind carries them into a house, and they crash to the ground. They meet Joanne and ask her about their map. She suggests asking her teacher.

Aims
- To teach *he's* and *she's*.
- To teach *here* and *there*.
- To teach some basic verbs.

Language
Oh no!
Help!
Hi.
Welcome.
Where's …?
He's/She's here.
He's/She's there.
Let's …
jump, hop, clap
place, teacher, ask, me, you

What you need
- CD and player.
- Optional: magazine pictures of people for "Before you begin."
- Optional: "paper bangers" for Exercise 1 (see *Extra activities*, page T83 in the Teacher's Book).

Before you begin

You could ask *Where's + (name of child)?* Teach *He's here* or *She's here* as appropriate. Do this a few times, so that the children begin to notice the difference between *he* and *she*.

Then point to a child on the other side of the room and teach *He's there* and *She's there*. The children then ask other children in the class, for example: *Diana, where's Tony?* If you have a single sex class, you could do this with magazine pictures of people stuck on different parts of the board. Give each person a name.

STUDENT'S BOOK

1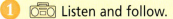

LISTENING TO THE STORY Before the children look at the story, you could ask them to close their books and listen. They will hear the sounds of the story and they should understand some of the language. This will stimulate their imagination and interest.

- *With the mother tongue:* Ask the children what they think happened. What did the balloon crash into? Why? Are Jess and Nick hurt? How is Kip feeling?
- *Without the mother tongue:* Pause the recording after each picture and get the children to tell you any words they hear.

Play the recording again while the children look at their books. Ask them about the characters in the story: *Where's Joanne?*, etc. The children point to the pictures and answer *She's here* or *He's here*.

ACTING OUT Play the recording once or twice again. The children then say the dialog in pairs or threes with their books open.

Ask them to close their books and try to say it again in pairs or threes. You can provide prompts on the board to help:

1 A town!   2 Help!   3 Welcome! My name's …   4 Jess?   5 Kip?   6 Where's this place?

Ask some children to act out the story for the class. There are three speaking parts (Jess, Nick, and Joanne) and a silent Kip. If the children have made paper bangers (see *Extra activities*, page T83 in the Teacher's Book), they can be used to dramatize the balloon crash.

EXTRA IDEA At a suitable time, you could get the class to make "animal ears" (see *Extra activities*, page T83 in the Teacher's Book). Whenever they are acting out the story, children playing the part of Kip can wear dog ears.

Classroom language and answer key

Listen.
Where are they?
What's that?

Where's …?

Who wants to act out the story?
Very good!
Well done!

2A • Where are we?

Where's Nick? Where's ...?

*Stand up.
Listen. Do the actions.*

Answers

```
d f d f h o p f g d
y s i t d o w n g m
c l a p n c a q q t
l d r a w y g h b e
f d r a s i n g t h
j h u e t f c v s k
g t e z w v j u m p
s t a n d u p j a g
j k q l p t s t w r
u j h i y w r i t e
```

Answers

2 She's here. 3 He's here.
4 She's here. 5 It's here.

Answers

2 seven 3 farm 4 cake
5 three 6 ten 7 four

2 Ask your friend. Find and say. **10 minutes**

Ask some children where the characters are. Encourage complete answers: *He's there. She's there.* Individual children can then ask other children.

They then work in pairs to ask each other. Go around and help as necessary.

EXTRA IDEAS
- Reinforce the difference between *here* and *there* by asking individuals about other children who are either nearby or on the other side of the room: *Helen, where's Richard?* (*He's here.*) *Richard, where's Maria?* (*She's there.*)
- You can make the pair work more fun and more memorable if the children use their binoculars from *Welcome!* C. Alternatively, they can make a paper "screen" about half the size of the page, with a hole in it about 1 cm across. Using the binoculars or screen, they can "search" the picture and say *He's/She's there!* when they find each character.
- Pairs could also use the screen to "search" the large picture on page 6. One child places the screen over the picture and the other asks, for example, *Where's the pen?* Once the first child has found a pen, he/she can say *It's there!*

Further practice: Activity Book Exercise 2.

3  Sing a song. **10 minutes**

This is an action song, so the children need to stand up. Play the recording and get the children to do the actions for each verse with you. Then play it again and get them to sing along with the song.

EXTRA IDEAS
- You can extend the song with other verbs that the children can mime/perform, for example, *Write, Draw, Sit down, Stand up.* You could end with *Sing.*
- You can play "Simon says" (see page T81 in the Teacher's Book).

Further practice: Activity Book Exercise 1.

ACTIVITY BOOK

1 Find seven more actions. Draw lines. **10 minutes**

New language: sit down, stand up

Before the children do the puzzle, go through the verbs. *Draw, write,* and *sing* have not been directly presented in the Student's Book, but the children will have seen and heard them in exercise instructions. This would also be a good opportunity to play "Simon says" (see *Extra activities,* page T81 in the Teacher's Book).

2 Write *He's, She's,* or *It's.* Draw lines. **10 minutes**

For practice with pronouns, you could start by putting Vocabulary Cards of the four characters, or of three or four objects, in different places around the walls. Ask the question *Where's ...?* Children point and answer *He's/She's/It's there.*

Then go through the exercise orally with the children before they complete it.

3 Write the words. **15 minutes**

When they have filled in the words, the children draw a picture to illustrate *teacher.* Be prepared for some unflattering pictures!

2 Ask your friend. Find and say.

Kip   Jess   Joanne   Nick   King Cat

Where's … ?
He's there!
She's there!

3 Sing a song.

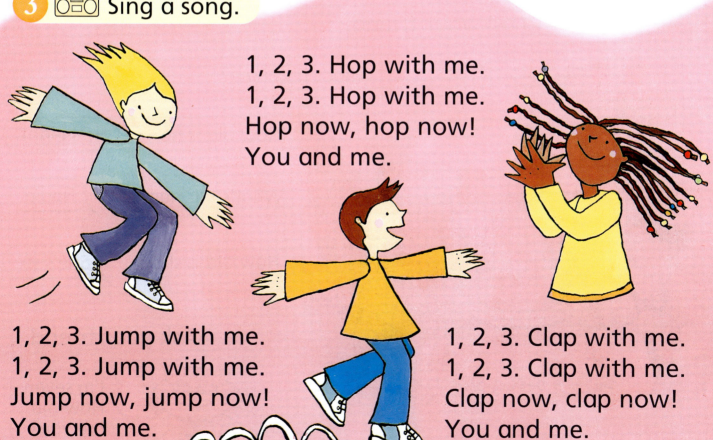

1, 2, 3. Hop with me.
1, 2, 3. Hop with me.
Hop now, hop now!
You and me.

1, 2, 3. Jump with me.
1, 2, 3. Jump with me.
Jump now, jump now!
You and me.

1, 2, 3. Clap with me.
1, 2, 3. Clap with me.
Clap now, clap now!
You and me.

2B King Cat's corner

1 Count with me.

"Look! A birthday party! How old is Steve?"

"One, two, three, four, five, six, seven, eight … He's eight!"

2 Point and ask your friend.

"What's his name?" — "Steve."

"How old is he?" — "He's eight."

"What's her name?" — "Nadia."

"How old is she?" — "She's six."

3 Ask your friend.

"I'm seven. How old are you?"

2B • King Cat's corner

Topic
King Cat provides puzzles, exercises, and a chant.

Aims
- To teach the children to ask how old someone is, and to say their age.
- To teach the numbers 10–15.
- To teach *his*, *her*, and *our* (for recognition only).

Language
birthday party
How old is Steve? He's …
How old is he/she? He's/She's …
How old are you? I'm …
What's his/her name?
Numbers 10–15
(Six) and (seven) are …
We're here.
our

What you need
- CD and player.

Before you begin

You could organize a class celebration for any of the children who have their birthday soon. As with many other countries, people in English-speaking countries generally celebrate birthdays with cards and a cake (with candles to show the age), by singing *Happy Birthday,* and by giving gifts. Many children have a birthday party in which organized games are often played. Some examples are:

- *Pass the parcel:* A small prize is wrapped up in many layers of paper. The parcel is passed from child to child in a circle while music is playing. Each time the music is stopped, the person holding the parcel removes one layer of paper. This continues until someone finds the prize.
- *Treasure hunt:* In teams, the children are given a series of clues to find a prize. See *Extra activities*, page T81 in the Teacher's Book.
- *Musical statues:* The children have to keep moving while music is played. They have to stand still as soon as the music stops. Any child who continues to move has a sticker put on him/her. The winner is the one who has the fewest stickers at the end.

STUDENT'S BOOK

Classroom language and answer key

1   **Count with me.** 10 minutes

You could start by teaching *How old are you? I'm …* Ask a few children how old they are, and help them to say their age in English. Get some children to ask others.

*How old are you?
Ask …*

Look at the picture with the children. Point to the boy in the middle and say *This is Steve. It's his birthday. How old is he?* and ask the children to count the candles on the cake. Then say *He's eight.*

*This is Steve.
It's his birthday.
How old is he?*

Read the sentences to the children. Then play the recording and encourage the children to count aloud along with King Cat. If they have made cat ears (see *Extra activities*, page T83 in the Teacher's Book), they could wear them here.

Listen.

2 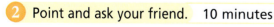 **Point and ask your friend.** 10 minutes

*What's his/her name?
How old is he/she?*

Ask the children to look at the picture. Point at each character, ask *What's his/her name?* and then supply the answer, for example, *This is Sam.* Ask *How old is he?* and elicit the answer *He's eight.* Ask about all the characters in the picture.

Put the class in pairs and get them to ask and answer.

*Work in pairs.
Ask your neighbor.*

3  **Ask your friend.** 5 minutes

*Work in a group.
Ask/Answer the question.*

The children now work in small groups. If you didn't teach *How old are you?/ I'm …* in Exercise 1, you should do that first. In their groups, the children take turns asking and answering each other.

2B • King Cat's corner

Count the candles.
Write the number.

How many candles are there?
Work in pairs.
Ask your friend.

Listen.
Say the number.

Look. What's the answer?

Read the number problems.
Write the answers.
Write a number problem.

Listen.
Say the sentence.
Say it again.

Answers
He's nine.
She's thirteen.

Answers
house, cat

4 Say the numbers. 10 minutes

Teach the word *candle*. Point to one in the picture or draw one on the board.

The children count the candles and write the number in figures above each cake. If you don't want them to write in their books, they can copy the number words into their notebooks, add the figures, and draw candles for each number.

Point at each cake, ask *How many candles are there?* and give the number. In pairs, the children can then ask each other *How many candles?* To practice the pronunciation, play the recording and ask the children to repeat.

EXTRA IDEA Draw a large circle on the board and write the numbers 1–15 inside it in random order. A child comes to the board, closes his/her eyes, and points somewhere inside the circle. He/She then names another child who has to say the number. The second child comes to the board, and so the game continues.

5 What's the answer? Write some more sums. 15 minutes

Before you ask the children to do the exercise, write some similar written sums on the board (e.g. *Nine and five are … Ten and three are …*) and elicit the answers.

Working alone or in pairs, the children write answers for the sums in their books. They could then write three or four more and give them to each other to answer.

EXTRA IDEA Make a simple worksheet of math sums with the numbers 1–15. If you write the sums in figures, the children can write the words underneath and then write the answers.

Further practice: Activity Book Exercises 1, 2, and 3.

6 Chant with me! 10 minutes

This chant reinforces the correct use of *he* and *she*. Play the recording through, and then sentence by sentence. Encourage the children to chant with the rhythm. As you come to the name *Daniel*, point at someone in the class and say his/her name instead.

EXTRA IDEA Substitute objects in the chant, reinforcing vocabulary from Unit 1. For example: *We're here/In our classroom/But where's the door?/It's here!*

ACTIVITY BOOK

1 Use the stickers (page St.1). 10 minutes

Look at the stickers with the children and ask them to count the candles on each cake. Then read through the sentences with them and ask where each sticker goes. Check that they have chosen the correct stickers before they stick them in place. They then complete the sentences for Simon and Martha.

2 How old are you? Draw your cake and candles. 20 minutes

The children draw their own cake with the appropriate number of candles for their last birthday, and complete the sentence. Encourage them to draw unusual shapes – animals, cars, spaceships, etc. If the children draw their cake on a separate piece of paper, you could make an attractive display on the wall.

3 Connect the dots. Write the words. 10 minutes

Read through the numbers with the children before they complete the puzzle.

4 🔊 Say the numbers.

ten eleven twelve thirteen fourteen fifteen

5 What's the answer? Write some more sums.

Six and seven are ….thirteen.…. Four and eight are …………………

Ten and four are ………………… Nine and six are …………………

Seven and ………………… are eleven. ………………… and four are fifteen.

6 🔊 Chant with me!

We're here
In our classroom,
But where's … *Daniel*?
He's HERE!

We're here
In our classroom,
But where's … *Sally*?
She's HERE!

We're here
In our classroom,
But where's …?

2C • We're here!

Topic
Joanne takes Nick and Jess to see her classroom. Kip wants to attack a mouse – which turns out to be Joanne's pencil case. The teacher shows the children where they are on the map.

Aims
- To teach *Yes, it is. / No, it isn't.*

Language
This is my …
That's my …
It's big.
It's a …
Yes, it is.
No, it isn't.
Good morning.
Where are we?
We're here.
What's number 1?
pencil case, desk, teacher, mouse

What you need
- CD and player.
- Optional: if possible, a furry pencil case for Exercise 1.
- The children will need their spinners for Activity Book Exercise 3.

Before you begin
- *With the mother tongue:* Ask the children what they remember about the story. Show Vocabulary Card 30 (Joanne) and ask her name. Ask how Jess and Nick met her (their balloon crashed), what they asked her (if she could understand the map), and what idea she suggested (to ask her teacher).
- *Without the mother tongue:* You could begin by saying the chant from Section B again. This will help review the use of *he* and *she*.

STUDENT'S BOOK

1 Listen and follow. 20+ minutes

LISTENING TO THE STORY Ask the children to close their books, and play the recording.

- *With the mother tongue:* You could then ask some questions: *Where are they? (In a classroom.) What did Kip see? (A mouse.) Was it really a mouse? (No. It was Joanne's pencil case.) Who is Mrs. Dell? (Joanne's teacher.) What did they ask Mrs. Dell? (Where they are on the map.)*
- *Without the mother tongue:* Pause the recording after each picture and ask the children what words they can understand.

Play the recording again for the children to follow in their books. Point at things in the pictures and ask questions, for example: *What's this? (It's a pencil case / a desk / a map.) Is this a mouse? (No, it isn't.) Who's this? (Mrs. Dell.)*

ACTING OUT Play the recording once or twice again. With their books open, the children can then say the dialog in groups of five (Nick, Jess, Joanne, Mrs. Dell, and sound effects for Kip).

Ask them to close their books and try to say it again in their groups. You could put some prompts in words on the board or, preferably, in pictures, to help them remember:
1 a desk   2 a mouse   3 a pencil case   4 a teacher   5–6 a map
7 Let's go! (in words)

Some children can act out the dialog for the class. If you have a furry pencil case, they can use it in their performance.

Classroom language and answer key

Close your books.
Listen.

Open your books.
Listen again.

Work in a group.
You are Nick/Jess (etc.).

Look at the board.

Who wants to act out the story?
Very good! Well done!

2C • We're here!

Answers
1 It's a cake. 2 It's a banana.
3 It's a desk. 4 It's a cat.
5 It's a mouse.
6 It's a pencil case.

2 Think. Find six things and say the words.   10 minutes

The children can work in pairs to find the six objects hidden in the picture. Check by asking what each object is. Then get them to take turns choosing a number and asking their partner what the object is.

EXTRA IDEA You could play "I spy" with the objects in the pictures (see *Extra activities*, page T80 in the Teacher's Book).

Further practice: Activity Book Exercise 1.

3 Listen and say.   10 minutes

First, teach *Yes, it is.* and *No, it isn't.* Point at one of the objects in Exercise 2 and say *It's a pencil case.* Teach *Yes, it is.* and repeat with a few more objects. Now make incorrect statements about some of the objects and teach *No, it isn't. It's a …*

Ask the children to look at the pictures. Check that they know the name of each object. Ask *What's this?* and elicit *It's a …*

Play the recording. Pause after each sentence for the children to answer either *Yes, it is.* or *No, it isn't. It's a …*

Answers
3 No, it isn't. It's a car.
4 No, it isn't. It's a house.
5 Yes, it is.
6 No, it isn't. It's a dog.

Tapescript 1
1 It's a bag.   2 It's a pencil.   3 It's a bus.   4 It's a school.
5 It's a book.   6 It's a cat.

Further practice: Activity Book Exercises 2 and 3.

ACTIVITY BOOK

1 Write the words.   10 minutes

The clues reveal the word *mouse* in the puzzle. When the children have filled it out, they write the word *mouse* and complete the drawing.

Answers
2 school 3 bus 4 desk
5 pencil

2 Read and write.   15 minutes

Go through the exercise orally with the children before you ask them to write their answers.

Answers
3 Yes, it is. 4 No, it isn't.
It's a dog. 5 Yes, it is.
6 No, it isn't. It's a mouse.

3 Play a game. Use your spinner. Color the board.   10 minutes

Note: This exercise has to be done in class. The children need their spinners.

The exercise reviews vocabulary in the form of a pair work game, using the spinners that the children made in *Welcome!* C (see teaching notes on the Activity Book on page T9). When they spin their spinner and land on a number, they have to answer a question, say a number, or say the word for an action. Before or after playing the game, they can color in the pictures.

2 Think. Find six things and say the words.

What's number 1? It's a ...

3 🔊 Listen and say.

1 It's a bag. Yes, it is.

2 It's a pencil. No, it isn't! It's a ruler.

3 It's a bus.

4 It's a school.

5 It's a book.

6 It's a cat.

2D The magic hat

1 🎧 Listen and follow.

2D • Storytime: The magic hat

Topic
Karen and Jack find a hat in the street. It is a magic hat and it makes Karen invisible. They go to school and Karen frightens everyone in the class. Then, a wizard appears – it is his hat.

Aims
- To develop the children's listening and speaking fluency.
- To review some of the language presented in Units 1 and 2.

Language
Review
Where's …?
It's a …
She isn't here.
What's that?
It's her bag.

New language
Wow!
I like …
Stop!
Where are you?
magic hat, spider

What you need
- CD and player.
- Optional: a ready-made magic hat for Exercise 2.
- For each child, markers and a piece of paper 50 x 50 cm for Exercise 2.
- Optional: some "wizard" clothes or a mask for Exercise 3.

Note: See the important note about Storytime units at the beginning of Section 1D of this Teacher's Book.

Before you begin

You could change the order of the exercises and make the magic hat (Exercise 2) first. This will stimulate the children's interest in the story.

STUDENT'S BOOK

1 Listen and follow.   10 minutes

Classroom language and answer key

You could use one of these approaches:
- *With the mother tongue:* Ask the children to close their books. Explain the title of the story to them and play the recording through. Then play it again in sections. Before the dialog for pictures 1–3, say *Listen. They're in the street.*, and before the dialog for pictures 4–7 say *Listen. They're in the classroom.* Ask the children to say what they think is happening, using their mother tongue. Encourage them to use their imagination.
- *Without the mother tongue:* Ask the children to look at the pictures. Point to different things and ask questions, supplying some of the answers as necessary. For example: *What's that?* (*A hat/house/street/bag/classroom, etc.*) *Where's Karen?* (*She's here.*) Look, she's invisible. *Where's the bag?* (*It's here.*) The bag's invisible, too. *Who's that? He's a wizard!*

Look at the pictures.
What can you see?
What's that?
Where's …?
Who's that?

The children can now follow the story in their books as you play the recording. Demonstrate the meaning of *I like …* by picking up various objects in the class and admiring them (*I like this bag. I like that book.*, etc.).

Listen.
Follow the words.

Divide the class into pairs. The children read alternate parts in the story from the book. Go around the class, listening and helping.

Work in pairs.
Read the story together.

T24

2D • The magic hat

Hold the paper like this.
Fold the paper like this.
Follow me.
Color your hat.
Put it on!

2 Make a magic hat. 20+ minutes

It is a good idea to show the children a completed hat before they begin. Make sure that each child has a large sheet of paper, and then make the hat with them. Follow the steps shown in the book, checking at each step that everyone has followed your instructions. They can then color the hat with stars, etc.

You may want to prepare some of the materials beforehand, although, ideally, the more the children do themselves, the better (remember, they are learning a lot more than just English in these activities). Some things you can consider:

- If you use a larger sheet of paper, should the children cut it down to 50 x 50 cm, or will you? (If they do the cutting, make sure they use children's scissors with rounded blades.)
- Should you make folds in the paper to help the children?
- Will the children color the hat or can you supply stickers of stars and other shapes?

3 Act out the story. Use your magic hat. 10 minutes

Who wants to act out the story?
You are Jack. You are Karen. (etc.)

You can now ask some children to act out the story for the class. There are five parts: Karen, Jack, teacher, wizard, and the class in picture 5. If you have some clothes or a mask for the wizard, that will add to the fun. To give some help, you can put prompts on the board:

1 Wow! – hat!   2 Karen! Where …?   3 magic   4 Where's your friend?
5 her bag   6 Help!   7 Where's …?

ACTIVITY BOOK Review

Note: You may prefer to use this material after you have done the Review section in the Student's Book.

1 Where are they? Write your answers. Draw lines. 15 minutes

Answers
Jess: She's here. Joanne: She's here. Nick: He's here. King Cat: He's here. Mrs. Dell: She's here.

Explain to the children that they have to find the characters in the picture. They draw lines to them and write the answers to the questions. Go through the questions first, getting them to trace lines to the characters with their finger.

2 Find the way. 10 minutes

Answers
How old are you? I'm (age).

The children have to find the correct way through the maze. This spells out a question, and they can then write their answer.

I can … 5 minutes

Before the children color in the stars, go through a few examples with them. Write the numbers 1–15 on the board, point to them in random order and get the children to say them. Ask *Where's …?* about different children in the class and elicit *He's/She's here.* Hold up a few objects (pencil, bag, eraser, etc.). Ask *Is it a …?* and get the children to reply *Yes, it is* or *No, it isn't*.

Picture Dictionary 2

Answers
1 This is Sally. She's eleven.
  This is Vincent. He's eleven.
  This is Susi. She's eight.
  This is David. He's ten.
  This is Pam. She's twelve.
2 fourteen; twelve; fifteen; ten; fifteen; thirteen

The children can now complete Picture Dictionary 2 on page 27. First, look at the stickers with them and check that they know where to stick them.

EXTRA PRACTICE There are optional *Extra practice* exercises for this unit on pages T92 and T93 in the Teacher's Book.

Review

1 🔊 Listen and write 1–4.

a

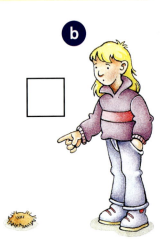
b

c

d

2 🔊 Play Bingo. Choose two cards.

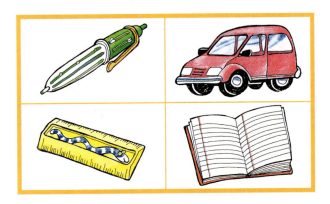

3 Play the game with your spinner.

Review

Topic
This section contains review exercises and a board game.

Aim
- To review the language covered in Units 1 and 2.

Language
Review
Useful phrases
Names of objects
Some verbs
It isn't a …

What you need
- CD and player.
- Small pieces of paper or posterboard for Exercise 2.
- The children need their spinners for Exercise 3.
- Game pieces or coins for Exercise 3.

STUDENT'S BOOK

1 Listen and write 1–4.   5 minutes

Before you play the recording, ask the children to look at the pictures. What do they think each child is saying?

Play the recording. The children have to listen and write the correct number (1–4) in the box for each picture.

> **Tapescript**
> 1 What's that?
> 2 How old is Steve?
> 3 What's nine and six?
> 4 Where's my pen?!

Classroom language and answer key

*Listen.
Write the number 1, 2, 3, or 4.*

Answers
a 4   b 1   c 2   d 3

2 Play Bingo. Choose two cards.   10 minutes

The children will each need eight small pieces of paper to cover the pictures as they hear the names of the objects.

To give them a practice run, ask them to choose just one card. Read out the words on the tapescript, but in a different order. The first person to cover a card completely is the winner.

Then ask the children to choose two new cards. Play the recording. The first person to cover two cards completely is the winner.

For more "Bingo" suggestions, see *Extra activities*, page T80 in the Teacher's Book.

> **Tapescript**
> a pen   a house   a cake   a dog   a notebook   a school   a banana   a drink
> a ruler   a bus   a sweet   a cat   a car   a sandwich   a bag
> a classroom

Let's play "Bingo."

*Choose a card.
Listen.
Put a paper on the picture.
Say "Bingo!" if you complete the card.
Now choose two cards.*

T26

Review

3 Play the game with your spinner. 20+ minutes

For this game, the children will need the spinners that they made in *Welcome!* C (see teaching notes on the Activity Book on page T9). They will each need a game piece or a coin to show where they are on the board.

Divide the class into pairs or threes and explain how to play the game.

1. Everyone puts their game piece on *Start*.
2. The players take turns spinning their spinners and moving the game pieces forward according to the number they get when it lands. They should say this number, and count their moves forward aloud.
3. When they land on a tile, they have to follow an instruction or answer a question. If they can't do it, the others in the group can help (there is no penalty for not knowing the answer).
4. The tiles with arrows mean "Go forward" or "Go back" the number of tiles shown on the arrow.
5. To finish, a player must land on *Finish* with the exact number. If the spinner shows a number that is too big to finish, the player counts into *Finish* and back out again.

3 Hello, Zara!

3A It's cold!

1 🔊 Listen and follow.

Act it out!

3A • It's cold!

Topic
Jess, Nick, and Joanne are back in the balloon. It's very cold, and it starts to snow. They decide to go down, but Nick thinks he sees two bears on the ground …

Aims
- To practice *be* questions.
- To teach short answers.

Language
Are you cold?
I'm very cold. I'm not.
Yes, I am. Yes, they are.
Yes, he/she is.
No, he/she isn't.
Is he in a balloon/car?
very, cold, snow, in, bear, dangerous, kick, down, round, in

What you need
- CD and player.
- Optional: small pieces of white paper for "snow" in Exercise 1.
- Optional: a large box for Exercise 1.

Before you begin
- *With the mother tongue:* Before you move into this next unit, ask the children what they can remember about Jess, Nick, Kip, and Joanne.
- *Without the mother tongue:* You could replay the recording from Unit 2C Exercise 1, to refresh their memory. You could also sing the balloon song from *Welcome!* C (page 9).

STUDENT'S BOOK

** 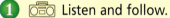**

You could start by teaching *Are you cold?* and the opposite, *Are you hot?* Mime *It's cold!* (shivering) or *It's hot!* (wiping sweat from your forehead). Then ask a few children *Are you cold? / Are you hot?* eliciting *Yes, I am* or *No, I'm not*. You can then add *very*. Mime *very cold / very hot*, and ask similar questions.

LISTENING TO THE STORY The children can have their books open or closed as you prefer. Play the recording but pause after the first two pictures. Ask the children *What's wrong?* or *What's the problem?* (*Nick's cold.*) or *Is Nick cold?* (*Yes, he is. He's very cold.*). Then ask *Why?* and, pointing at the snow, say *Look, there's snow.* (Note that *There is/are* is taught in Unit 3C – here it is just for recognition.) Translate *snow* or mime snowflakes falling.

Play the recording for the next two pictures and again ask *What's wrong?* or *What's the problem?* Point at the two bears in the picture and say *Look. There are two bears.* Illustrate, mime, or translate *bear*. Ask *What's the problem with bears?* Say *They're dangerous* and mime or translate *dangerous*.

Finally, play the recording for the last two pictures. Then play it all the way through, while students listen with their books open.

ACTING OUT First, divide the class into pairs or groups of three and get the children to read the parts of the dialog.

Ask some children to act out the story (there are four parts: Jess, Nick, Joanne, and Kip). As the text is longer here, they can read from their books, or you could write the dialog on the board. Alternatively, provide some prompts:

1 Brr! 2 Snow! 3 What's that? 4 Two bears! 5 cold – dangerous 6 What now?

To make the acting more fun, the children could stand in a box representing the balloon basket. You could also use pieces of white paper as pretend snow.

Classroom language and answer key

Are you cold/hot?
Yes, I am. No, I'm not.

Open your books to page 28.
Close your books.
Listen.
What's the problem?
Listen to the next part.

Listen again.

Work in pairs/threes.
Read the words.

Who wants to act it out?
I need three children.
Come to the front of the class.
You are … You are …
Very good!
Excellent!

3A • It's cold!

Answers
2 Nadia is in a classroom.
3 Sue is in a park.
4 Maria is in a house.
5 Sam is in a car.
6 Steve is in a bus.

Look at the pictures.
Find the answer.

Listen and answer.

2 Where are they?   10 minutes

This exercise prepares the children for Exercise 3. First, check that they know the words for the objects on the right in the picture.

Ask *Where's Daniel?* and elicit *He's in a balloon.* The children then work in pairs to find out where the other people are.

3 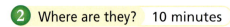 Listen and answer.   5 minutes

You could first read the questions in the tapescript for the children to reply. You could then play the recording and pause after each question so they can reply again.

> **Tapescript 1**
> 1 Is Daniel in a balloon? Yes, he is.   2 Is Nadia in a bus? No, she isn't. She's in a classroom   3 Is Sue in a park? Yes, she is.   4 Is Maria in a car? No, she isn't. She's in a house.   5 Is Sam in a car? Yes, he is.
> 6 Is Steve in a balloon? No, he isn't. He's on a bus.

Further practice: Activity Book Exercises 2 and 3.

4 Sing a song.   10 minutes

Read through the words with the children and get them to do the actions. Then play the recording, and get them to sing it while they do the actions:

Let's sing.
Do the actions.

(sitting down)
Up (point up) and down (point down)
Big (outstretched arms) and small (hands closed)
Round and round (hands in a circle)
Stand up tall! (stand up straight)

(now standing up)
Up (point up) and down (point down)
Big (outstretched arms) and small (hands closed)
Round and round (turn around)
Kick a ball! (kick an imaginary ball)

Further practice: Activity Book Exercise 1.

ACTIVITY BOOK

Answers
2 small   3 up   4 cold
5 big   6 down

1 Draw lines.   10 minutes

New language: hot
The children join each word to the correct picture.

Answers
Penguin: Yes, it is. No, it isn't.
Lion: No, it isn't. Yes, it is.

2 Look at the picture. Answer the questions.   15 minutes

New language: penguin, lion
Read through the questions with the children and listen to their answers. The first part of the exercise prepares them for the second part.

Answers
A rabbit isn't dangerous.
It isn't very big. It isn't in a cold place.

3 Use the stickers (page St.2).   15 minutes

New language: polar bear, rabbit
The children first stick the pictures of a polar bear and a rabbit onto the page. Read through the text about the polar bear with them. Then ask about the rabbit. Write the sentences on the board, read them aloud, and then wipe them off. The children can then write about the rabbit by themselves.

2 Where are they?

Daniel is in a balloon.

Daniel
Nadia
Sue
Maria
Sam
Steve

3 Listen and answer.

Is Daniel in a balloon?

Is Nadia in a bus?

Yes, he is.

No, she isn't! She's in a ...

4 Sing a song.

Up and down, Big and small.

Round and round,
Stand up tall!
La la la la la!

Up and down,
Big and small.
Round and round,
Kick a ball!
La la la la la!

29

3B King Cat's corner

1 🔊 Point and say the colors.

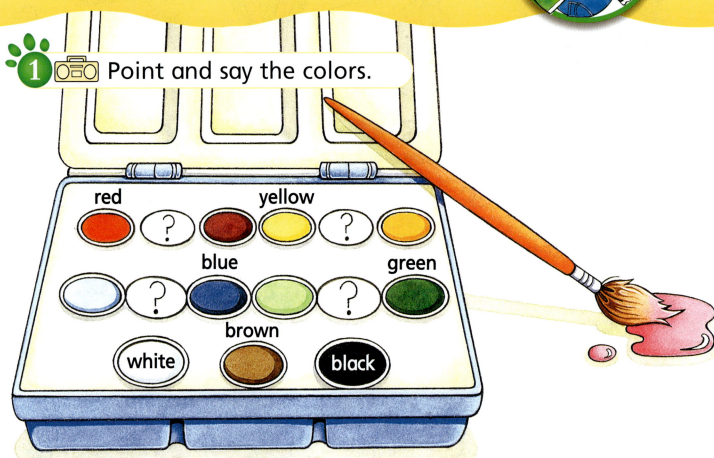

2 Think. Where are these colors? Point and say.

It's yellow. It's here!

3 Think. What's wrong?

The dog is green!

3B • King Cat's corner

Topic
King Cat helps the children practice.

Aims
- To teach the names of the colors.
- To teach some adjectives.
- To teach the use of *they are/aren't*.

Language
The dog is green!
favorite
Blue's our favorite color.
Are they …?
Yes, they are.
No, they aren't.
red, green white, brown, yellow, blue, black
big, small

What you need
- CD and player.
- Colored white board markers or colored chalk for "Before you begin."
- If the children wear a uniform, bring some items of different colors for "Before you begin."

Before you begin

You can make the presentation of colors interesting if you personally involve the students. Say *Look at the colors in our classroom! Red, yellow, green* (etc.). Point at the different colors that the children are wearing, or use the colored items that you have brought in.

Write the names of the colors on the board with the colors beside them. Say *(Color) is my favorite color. Look.* Point and say the color a few times. Ask a few children *What's your favorite color?*

STUDENT'S BOOK

1 **Point and say the colors.**   10 minutes

Ask the children to open their books and to look at the picture. Play the recording. As they hear each word, the children point at the appropriate color.

> **Tapescript**
> Blue. Green. Yellow. Red. Black. White. Brown.

2 **Think. Where are these colors? Point and say.**   3 minutes

The children now decide where each of the colors are in the paint box – that is, whether it is one of the reds, the yellows, the blues, or the greens. Ask *Where is this color?* and elicit, for example, *It's red. It's here.*

3 **Think. What's wrong?**   5 minutes

Allow a few minutes for the children to work with their neighbor, deciding what they can say about each picture together. Then ask for their answers.

Classroom language and answer key

Listen. Point at the colors.

Answers
It's yellow. It's here.
It's green. It's here.
It's red. It's here.
It's blue. It's here.

What's wrong? Work in pairs.

Answers
The banana is blue. The drink is black and red and white. The cat is blue and green. The sandwich is yellow and black.

3B • King Cat's corner

> Listen.
> Chant with King Cat!
> Let's chant again.

4 Chant with me!   10 minutes

First, read the words through with the children. Point at things that are blue when you say *It's here. It's there.* Then play the recording and get the children to chant.

Repeat the chant without the recording, and choose a child to say *No, it isn't! It's ...*, replacing the color with a new one and pointing at an example.

EXTRA IDEA You could add a color each time, instead of replacing it. That way, the chant will get longer and longer:

Blue, green, yellow.
They're our favorite colors.
They're here. They're there.
Blue, green, yellow.

The use of plurals will connect well with Exercise 5.

Further practice: Activity Book Exercises 1 and 2.

5 Play a game. Choose three balls. Your friend can guess.   15 minutes

This exercise is intended to teach the plural form *Are they ...?* but you may like to review *Is it ...?* first. Say *Look at the picture. I'm thinking. I have a ball in my head* (tapping your head). Write up some example questions for guessing: *Is it big? Is it small? Is it green? Is it red?* The children then ask you questions to which you reply *No, it isn't* or *Yes, it is.*

When they have guessed the ball you chose, get a few children to choose one from the picture. The rest of the class ask questions to figure out which one it is.

You can now play the game in the same way, but this time say *I have three balls in my head.* Write plural questions on the board: *Are they big? Are they small?* (etc.) Get a few children to choose three balls and the rest of the class can ask and guess.

> Look at the picture.
> I'm thinking. I have a ball in my head.
> Ask me!

The children can now play the game in pairs. Go around the class and help as required.

Further practice: Activity Book Exercise 3.

> Now work in pairs.
> Choose and ask.

ACTIVITY BOOK

1 Color the picture. What is it?   10 minutes

The children have to read the names of the colors and color in each shape with the appropriate color.

> **Answer**
> It's a rabbit.

2 Make new colors   5 minutes

The children read the color names and color in the pots and the paints to make new colors. Teach *orange* and *purple*, and get the children to label the pictures. (Yellow + blue makes green. Yellow + red makes orange. Blue + red makes purple.)

3 Read the poem. Write the words.   10–15 minutes

Read the poem through with the children and get them to supply the missing words, using the pictures. They then write in the missing words. To help with this, you may like to put the words in random order on the board.

> **Answers**
> pencil, car, house,
> dog, cat, rabbit, bear,
> Snow, Cats, Bananas, Dogs

Get the class to read the poem together. They could do actions for the last line of each verse.

4 Chant with me!

Blue, blue, blue.
Blue's our favorite color.
It's here. It's there.
Blue, blue, blue.

No, it isn't! It's green!

5 Play a game. Choose three balls. Your friend can guess.

Are they big?
Are they green?
Are they red?
Yes, they are.
Are they small?
Are they blue?
No, they aren't.

3C Help!

1 🔊 Listen and follow.

1. Look! There's a house. And there's a girl on skis.
2. Let's yell! HELP! HELP! HELP!
3. Hello! My name's Zara. Come down. No! There are two bears!
4. They aren't bears! They're my dogs! NICK!
5. Look, Zara. That's the town. But what's this?
6. I know! Let's go!

Act it out!

3C • Help!

Topic
Nick, Jess, and Joanne are still in the balloon, frightened of the two bears below. They see a girl on skis and call for help. She comes over and they discover that the bears are not bears at all …

Aims
- To teach *There is* and *There are*.

Language
There's/There are
Let's yell!
Help!
They aren't
girl, skis, boy, tree, garden, strong

What you need
- CD and player.
- Some objects for "Kim's game" in "Before you begin."
- Optional: a box for Exercise 1.
- The children will need their spinners for Activity Book Exercise 2.

Before you begin
This section teaches *There is* and *There are*. Before you start, you could play "Kim's game" (see *Extra activities*, page T81 in the Teacher's Book) to introduce the structure naturally.

- Place six or seven objects on a table (e.g. a pen, pencil, eraser, bag, pencil case, book, and ruler). Point to each object and say what there is: *There's a pen. There's a pencil*, etc.
- Now cover the objects. Ask the children if they can remember what there is on the table. As they name something, encourage them to say it in a full sentence: *Yes, that's right! There's a …*
- Repeat the game. This time, add one or two more of some items and use *There are* as well as *There is*.

STUDENT'S BOOK

1 Listen and follow.   20+ minutes

Before the children look at their books, ask questions about what happened last time in the story and help the children to give complete answers. For example: *Where are the children?* (*In the balloon.*) *Are they hot or cold?* (*Cold.*) *Why?* (*There's snow.*) *What's the problem?* (*There are two bears.*) You could play the recording for Section A once again.

LISTENING TO THE STORY Ask the children to open their books. Play the recording but pause after the first two pictures. Ask *What is there?* Elicit *There's a house. There's a girl.* Play the recording for the next two pictures and ask *Are they bears?* Elicit *No, they aren't. They're dogs.*

Draw attention to the two different forms here, *There are* and *They are*. If possible, explain the difference in meaning in the mother tongue, but otherwise write the phrases on the board and underline the difference. It is potentially confusing, but don't worry too much at this stage.

Finally, play the recording for the last two pictures, and then play it through.

ACTING OUT Divide the class into pairs or groups and get the children to read the parts of the dialog.

Ask some children to act out the story (there are five parts: Jess, Joanne, Nick, Zara, and a silent Kip). They can read from their books, you could write the dialog on the board, or simply supply some prompts:

1 a house – a girl   2 Let's yell!   3 No! There are two bears!
4 They're my dogs.   5 What's this?   6 Let's go!

To make it more fun, the children could stand in a large box for pictures 1–4 and then sit around a table for 5 and 6. They can have a sheet of paper as a map.

Classroom language and answer key

Open your books.
Listen.
What is there?
Are there bears?

Work in pairs/groups.
Read the words.

Who wants to act it out?
I need five children.
Come to the front.
Can you speak louder?
Excellent! Well done!

3C • Help!

Look. There's a ...

Look at picture 1/2.
Find the things.

Answers
1 There's a car.
   There's a bear.
   There are two boys.
   There's a girl.
   There are six houses.
2 There are four bears.
   There are three girls.

Look at the objects.
Draw a picture.
Tell us about your picture.

Let's read the words.
Listen and sing!

Answers
a There are six cars.
   There's a cat. There's a dog.
   There are two big houses.
b There are five cars.
   There are two cats.
   There are two dogs.
   There are two small houses.

2 Find the things. Then talk about the pictures. 15 minutes

Read through the names of the animals, people, and things. Point and say *Look. There's a bear. There's a car* (etc.).

Focus on the "story" in the pictures. You can ask questions: *Is it hot?* (*No, it isn't. It's cold. It's very cold.*) *Look at the dog! Is it a good dog?* (*No, it isn't.*) *Look at the car keys.* The word *keys* is new, but the meaning is clear from the pictures.

Ask the children to look first at picture 1 and then at picture 2, and to find the things from the list. They point and use *There is* or *There are*.

EXTRA IDEA Ask the children to close their books and play the memory game again. You can play it in different ways:
1 Say some sentences, for example, *There's a girl. There are four bears.* The children have to write down *1* or *2* depending on which picture contains these things.
2 Ask some questions: *In picture 2, how many bears are there? How many houses/boys/trees are there?*
3 The children write down as many things as they can remember about the pictures. Put two columns on the board:

   Picture 1   Picture 2
   There's a ...   There's a ...
   There are ...   There are ...

Further practice: Activity Book Exercise 1.

3 Draw a picture. Tell your friend. 15 minutes

This may take some time, so you may like to ask the children to draw their picture at home and to bring it to class on another day. They can draw any situation they like, but the picture should include the things and people from Exercise 2. When they have finished, ask individuals to tell the class about their picture.

4 Sing a song. 10 minutes

Read through the words with the children first, and then play the recording. Encourage them to sing along.

EXTRA IDEA You could divide the class into two. One half can sing the verses, and the other half can sing the chorus.

Further practice: Activity Book Exercise 2.

ACTIVITY BOOK

1 Think. Find four more differences. Write sentences. 10 minutes

Ask the children to tell you what differences they can see between the pictures. After they have said what they can see, you could put the key words on the board to help them in their writing: *dog, car, cat, house*.

2 Play a game. Use your spinner. Color the board. 10 minutes

Note: This exercise has to be done in class. The children need their spinners.

The exercise reviews language in the form of a game, using the spinners that the children made in *Welcome!* C (see teaching notes on the Activity Book on page T9). When they spin their spinner and land on a number, they have to answer a question or make a sentence with *He's, She's,* or *It's*.

2 Find the things. Then talk about the pictures.

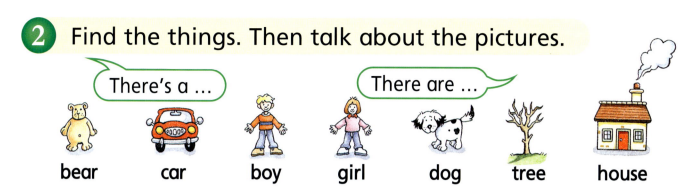

There's a …   There are …

bear   car   boy   girl   dog   tree   house

3 Draw a picture. Tell your friend.

4 🔊 Sing a song.

There's a dog in my garden
And his name is Woofity Woof!

Woof woof Woofity
Woof woof Woofity
Woof woof Woofity Woof

There's a dog in my garden
And he's big and strong.

There's a cat in my garden
But where's Woofity Woof?

3D • Storytime: Eddie elephant

Topic
A man is walking in the jungle. He is very hot and eventually collapses. Some elephants come to his aid by spraying him with water.

Aims
- To develop the children's listening and speaking fluency.
- To review language covered in earlier units.

Language

Review
I'm
It's
What's this?
What's that?
Come on!
hot, very, friend

New language
Can you help me?
Of course!
Thank you.
elephant, man, trumpet

What you need
- CD and player.
- Copies of Cut-out 5 (Teacher's Book, page T121) for Exercise 2.
- Scissors, glue, markers, and tape for Exercise 2.
- Optional: a ready-made elephant trumpet for Exercise 2.

Note: See the important note about Storytime units at the beginning of Unit 1D in the Teacher's Book.

Before you begin
You could decide to change the order of the exercises and make the elephant trumpet first.

STUDENT'S BOOK

1 **Listen and follow.**   15 minutes

You can start by telling the story. Ask the children to look at the pictures. Point to the pictures and slowly say what is happening. If you add some new words, you can make the story more interesting to listen to. It is not necessary for the children to understand every single word. A richer context for listening will help to develop their listening fluency. For example:

1 Look. There's a man. He's in the jungle. There's a tree. There are two monkeys. There's a snake. Hissssss! The man says, "I'm hot!"
2 He's very hot. He says, "I'm very hot!"
3 And now there's an elephant. Look. The elephant says, "What's this? It's a man!"
4 The man says, "I'm hot! I'm very hot! Can you help me?"
5 The elephant can help. He says, "Of course! Eeeeee!" (If you have a ready-made trumpet, use it here.)
6 Look. There are two elephants. This elephant says, "What's that?" and this elephant says, "It's Eddie, our friend. Come on!"
7 Look! They can help the man. Now he isn't hot!

Play the recording once or twice. The children follow the story in their books.

Divide the class into fours (the man, Eddie the elephant, and the other two elephants), and get them to read the dialog.

Classroom language and answer key

Listen to the story.
Look at the pictures.
Look at picture 1....

Listen.

Work together.
Read the story.

3D • Eddie elephant

> Hold the paper like this.
> Fold the paper like this.
> Follow me.
> Color your trumpet.

> Who wants to act out the story?
> You are the man.
> You are an elephant (etc.).

Answers
There are two bananas in the pencil case. There's a mouse in the bag. There are two rulers in the cake.

Example answers
1 blue 2 yellow 3 green
4 red, yellow, green

Answers
No, it isn't.
No, it isn't.

2 Make an elephant trunk. 10 minutes

Optional: Cut-out 5 (page T121 in the Teacher's Book)
Warning! The elephant trumpet makes a loud noise!

It is a good idea to show the children a completed trumpet before they begin. Make sure that each child has a copy of Cut-out 5 and make the trumpet with them.

Ideally, the more the children do themselves, the better. However, this craft activity requires the careful use of scissors. Some questions to consider:
- Should the children cut out the elephant face, or should you?
- Should they cut out the trunk, or should you?
- Should they glue the pieces together, or should you?

Make sure that the children use scissors with rounded blades.

3 Act out the story. Use your trunk to trumpet like an elephant. 10 minutes

You can now ask some children to act out the story (four parts). They can use their elephant trumpets when they get to picture 5 in the story.

ACTIVITY BOOK Review

1 Think. What's wrong? Write sentences. 20 minutes

You could use Vocabulary Cards 11–13, 24–26, and 31 to review vocabulary for this exercise. Talk about each picture with the children before they write.

2 Color the pictures. Write the names of the colors. 10 minutes

The children color the objects and write the names of the colors.

3 Answer the questions. 10 minutes

The children read the questions and write their answers.

I can … 5 minutes

Before the children color in the stars, look at the pictures with them. Get them to say the colors of the paint tins and what there is/are in the street.

Picture Dictionary 3

The children can now complete Picture Dictionary 3 on page 44.

EXTRA PRACTICE There are some optional *Extra practice* exercises for this unit on pages T94 and T95 in the Teacher's Book.

Answers
2 It isn't a pen. It's a house.   They aren't balls. They're cars.
   They aren't dogs. They're bears.   It isn't a cat. It's a mouse.   It isn't a ruler. It's a bag.
3 1 B   2 B   3 A   4 B
4 In Picture A there isn't a bus but in Picture B there's a bus.
   In Picture A there isn't a car but in Picture B there's a car.
   In Picture A there are nine houses but in Picture B there are eight houses.
   In Picture A there are five cats but in Picture B there are four cats.
   In Picture A there's one dog but in Picture B there are two dogs.
   In Picture A there are five balls but in Picture B there are six balls.

2) Make an elephant trunk.

You need: cut-out 5, scissors, glue, markers, tape

3) Act out the story. Use your trunk to trumpet like an elephant.

4 Hello, Tom!

4A The birds

1  Listen and follow.

Act it out!

4A • The birds

Topic
Jess, Joanne, Nick, and Zara are in the balloon. They are over a farm. Unfortunately, some birds attack the balloon and it plunges to the ground.

Aims
- To teach the meaning and use of *can* to express ability.
- To teach some more verbs.

Language
I can
What can we do?
We can
Go away!
cow, horse, bird
see, hear, yell, climb, fly, sing, write, swim, hop, clap, look at, read, count, jump

What you need
- CD and player.
- Optional: a large cardboard box for Exercise 1.
- Optional: "paper bangers" (see *Extra activities*, page T83 in the Teacher's Book), or pieces of cardboard to rip, for Exercise 1.

Before you begin
You could start by teaching the use of *can*, using one of these approaches:
- Look back at picture 3 in *Welcome!* C, page 8, and ask the children what they can see. Encourage complete sentences for their answers: *I can see a park*.
- Look out of the classroom window and ask the children what they can see: *Look! What can you see?* (*I can see a bird. I can see a tree*, etc.).
- Start with Exercise 3, which naturally introduces *can* in an action song.

STUDENT'S BOOK

 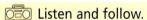 **Listen and follow.**   10 minutes

Ask the children some of the questions about the story so far, either in English or in the mother tongue.

LISTENING TO THE STORY The children can have their books open or closed when they listen. Play the recording and pause after pictures 1 and 2. Ask *What can Joanne/Jess see? What can Zara hear?* Say *Yes, Zara can hear birds. That's a problem! Why?* Answer the question yourself: *The birds can make the balloon go BANG!*

Then ask *What can they do?* Invite suggestions and supply *They can yell. What can they yell? Listen.* Play the recording for pictures 3 and 4. Say *Jess has an idea! What is it? Listen!*

Play the recording for picture 5. Ask *What can Jess do?* and elicit *She can climb.* Say *It's too late! Listen.* and play the recording for picture 6.

Finally, play the recording through. The children listen with their books open.

ACTING OUT Divide the class into pairs or groups of five and get them to read the dialog.

Ask some children to act out the story (five parts: Jess, Nick, Joanne, Zara, and Kip). They can read from their books, you could write the dialog on the board, or you could supply prompts:
1 a farm – cows and horses   2 birds. Oh no!   3 What can we do?   4 Go away!
5 climb up   6 RRRIPPP!

As before, the children could stand in a box to simulate the balloon basket. You could take a piece of cardboard and rip it in half as the balloon explodes, and if the children have made "paper bangers," they could use those (see *Extra activities*, page T83 in the Teacher's Book).

Classroom language and answer key

Listen.
What can Joanne see?
What can Zara hear?

What can they do?

Open your books at page 36.
Listen again.

Work in pairs/groups.
Read the words.

Who wants to act out the story?
I need four children.
Come to the front.
Excellent! Great!

4A • The birds

Answers
b I can write. c I can hear.
d I can sing. e I can climb.
f I can fly. g I can see.
h I can swim.

② Match the pictures and the sentences. 8 minutes

Establish the meaning of each sentence by getting the children to stand up and mime the actions with you. Repeat this a few times, and then ask them to match the pictures and sentences.

Further practice: Activity Book Exercises 1, 2, and 3.

③ 🔊 Listen and do the actions. 5 minutes

When you are sure that the children understand the verbs from Exercise 2, play the recording while the children mime the actions. This gradually gets faster!

Tapescript

Hello! I can do lots of things. [*repeat*]
Can you do them, too? And again!
I can climb and I can swim.
I can fly and I can yell. [*repeat*]
I can sing and I can hear. Phew!
I can see and I can write.
Let's do it again!

④ 🔊 Sing a song. 10 minutes

This is another action song. Read through the words with the children first and get them to do the actions. Then play the recording and get them to sing while they do the actions.

ACTIVITY BOOK

*Let's read the words first.
Do the actions with me.*

① Use the stickers (page St.2). 5 minutes

Help the children to find the correct stickers in the middle of the Activity Book. Before they stick the stickers, ask them to decide where they should go. They then write two verbs under each animal.

Answers
dog: jump, swim
bird: sing, fly
bear: climb, swim

② Write the name of the animal. 5 minutes

The children write the name of each animal.

Answers
A dog, A bird, A bear

③ What can you do? Check the boxes. 15 minutes

The children first check the boxes and then complete the sentence.

Answers
swim, climb, sing

④ Count and write. 10 minutes

To complete the sentence, the children need to count the animals and cars and then write the correct plural word in each blank.

Answers
two dogs, four cars, seven cows, eight horses, nine cats, and eleven birds.

2. Match the pictures and the sentences.

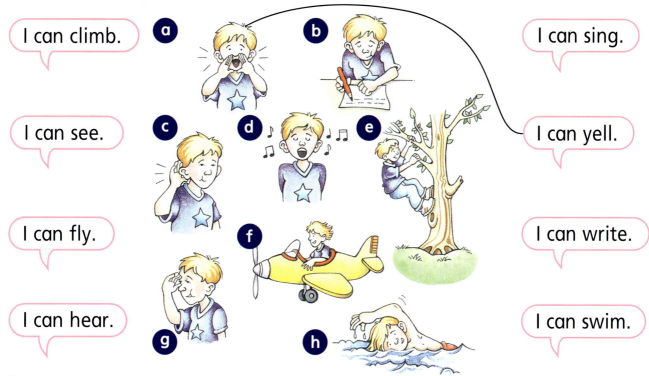

I can climb.
I can see.
I can fly.
I can hear.
I can sing.
I can yell.
I can write.
I can swim.

3. 🎧 Listen and do the actions.

4. 🎧 Sing a song.

I can hop
and I can see.
I can clap.
Just look at me!

I can read
and count to three.
I can jump.
Just look at me!
La la la la la!

4B King Cat's corner

1 Match the parts to make an animal. Find the word.

a horse   a cow   a bird   a dog   a bear   a cat

2 Here are some strange animals. Think. What are they?

It's a dog-bird!

3 Draw some strange animals. Ask your friend.

4B • King Cat's corner

Topic
King Cat helps the children to practice using animal words and to learn some new numbers.

Aims
- To review the names of animals.
- To teach the numbers 15–20.

Language
Numbers 15–20
everything
away
dinner time

What you need
- CD and player.
- Optional: copies of Cut-out 6 (Teacher's Book, page T122), cut into separate jigsaw puzzle pieces, for Exercise 1 "Extra ideas" and Exercise 2.
- Small pieces of paper for "Bingo" in Exercise 5.

Before you begin
You could take various approaches:
- Ask the children to look at Section A again. What animals can they see? Write the names on the board as they suggest them (cow, horse, dog, bird). Ask them to look back at Units 1–3 to find some more animals. Write up the names as they suggest them (a bear, a cat).
- Make some animal noises. The children have to guess the animal.
- Use Vocabulary Cards 20, 21, 31, 32, and 53–55 for the animals. Hold the cards up separately, and then two at a time to elicit, for example, *a horse and a bear*.

STUDENT'S BOOK

1 Match the parts to make an animal. Find the word. 8 minutes

Look at the pictures with the children and get them to tell you which animal they think each puzzle piece belongs to. They then draw lines to match the pieces to the correct word.

EXTRA IDEAS
- Beforehand, photocopy Cut-out 6 (page T122 in the Teacher's Book) and cut out the puzzle pieces. Hold up each piece and ask the children what animal they think it is. Then put the pieces face down on a table or, better, attach them face down to the board. When you show one piece, the children try to guess or remember where the matching piece is to make up a complete animal.
- Make this into a pair work memory game. Photocopy Cut-out 6 so that there is one set of puzzle pieces for every two children. In pairs, they spread the pieces out, face down. They take turns lifting up one piece and then another, trying to find a matching pair. If they find a match, they take both pieces. If the pieces don't match, they put them back, face down. The person with the most animals at the end is the winner.

2 Here are some strange animals. Think. What are they? 3 minutes

The children can suggest names for each animal. If you have made puzzle pieces from Cut-out 6, you can invent more "strange animals" on the board.

3 Draw some strange animals. Ask your friend. 15+ minutes

This may take some time in class, so it may be a good idea to ask the children to draw their pictures at home. Ask them to draw two or three strange "puzzle" animals like the ones in Exercise 2. They can then ask their neighbor or the class what the name of the animal is.

Classroom language and answer key

Look at the pictures.
Can you match the pictures?
What is the name?

Answers
It's a bird-dog. It's a cat-cow.

Think of an animal.
A strange animal.
Draw a picture.

4B • King Cat's corner

Write the numbers.

Listen. Say the numbers.
Repeat after me.
What's the number?

Let's play Bingo.
Choose a card.
Listen for the number.
Put a paper on the square.

Choose two cards.

Answers
a horse-cat/cat-horse
a bear-bird/bird-bear

Answers
see, cake
cat, hear, mouse
mouse, run, cat

4 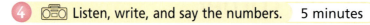 Listen, write, and say the numbers. **5 minutes**

First, allow the children to write the numbers 16–20 above the words. If you don't want them to write in their books, they can copy the words into their notebooks and write the numbers above them.

Read the numbers aloud and get the children to repeat. Then play the recording. Pause after each number and ask the children to say the next number before they hear it.

EXTRA IDEA You could write the numbers 10–20 around the board in random order. Close your eyes and point to a number, which the children then have to say.

5 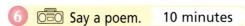 Write the numbers. Play Bingo. Choose two cards. **10 minutes**

This game practices the numbers 1–20. Before they play it, ask the children to count the number of small squares in each part of the four cards. Check that they can say and understand the numbers in English.

The children will need small pieces of paper to play the game. For a practice round, you could ask them to choose one card only. Read out numbers from the tapescript, but in a different order. If the children hear a number that they have on their card, they cover it with a piece of paper. The first person to cover their card completely is the winner.

The children now choose two cards to play the game. Play the recording.

> **Tapescript**
> Four, sixteen, six, nine, seven, eight, eleven, twelve,
> ten, fourteen, three, five, thirteen, eighteen, fifteen.

Further practice: Activity Book Exercise 1.

6 Say a poem. **10 minutes**

First, talk about the pictures with the children. Ask them some questions, for example:

- Picture 1: *Who's this? (King Cat.) What can he see? (A bird.) Where's the bird? (In the tree.) What can King Cat do? (He can climb the tree.)*
- Picture 2: *Where's King Cat now? (In the tree.) What can the bird do? (It can fly.)*

Read the poem out and then play the recording. The children can then read it aloud. If you divide the class in half, one half can be King Cat and the other half can be the bird.

Further practice: Activity Book Exercise 2.

ACTIVITY BOOK

1 Connect the dots. What are they? Write the words. **10 minutes**

Read through the numbers with the children so that they can review the words. They can point at each number with their fingers. Then they connect the dots and write the names of the two strange animals.

2 Read the poem. Write the words. **15 minutes**

New vocabulary: just for me, over there, near

Read through the poem with the children and get them to suggest the missing words. They then complete the poem with the words in the box.

🔊 Listen, write, and say the numbers.

15 ....
fifteen   sixteen   seventeen   eighteen   nineteen   twenty

 🔊 Write the numbers. Play Bingo. Choose two cards.

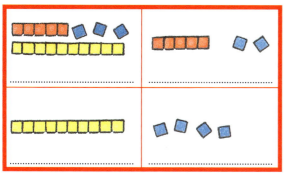
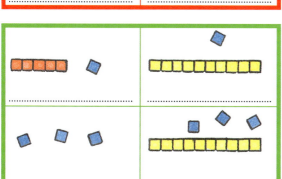
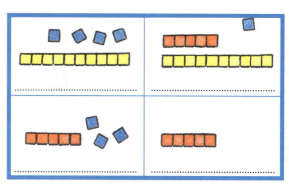
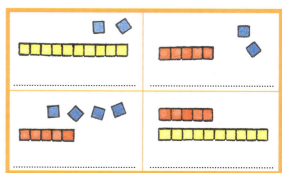

  Say a poem.

I'm a cat
And I can see
A bird up there
For me!

I'm a bird
And I can sing.
From my tree
I see everything.

I'm a bird
And I can fly
Away, away,
Up to the sky!

I'm a cat
And I can climb.
But where's that bird?
It's my dinner time!

 # I can help.

1 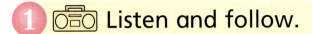 Listen and follow.

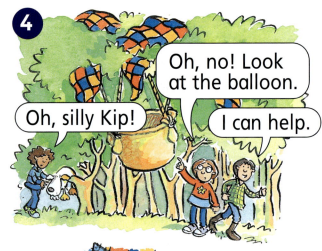

Act it out!

4C • I can help.

Topic
Jess, Joanne, Zara, and Nick have landed in a tree. They jump down and meet Tom. The balloon is ripped, so Tom finds things to repair it – but his parents aren't pleased!

Aims
- To teach the meaning and use of *can't* to describe ability.
- To teach the names of some farm animals.

Language
What can we do?
We can …
I can …, I can't …
Thanks.
(A horse) can/can't …
legs, silly, Mom, Dad, duck, hen, chick
walk, fly, swim, run fast, jump high

What you need
- CD and player.
- Optional: a blanket and a large box for Exercise 1.

Before you begin

Before you start, you could teach the use of *can't*. Ask the children what things they can do. Write some of their answers on the board, for example, *I can climb. I can see. I can shout.* They could look at page 37, Exercise 2 for more ideas.

Write *cat* and *bird* on the board, and ask what each animal can do. Elicit sentences such as *It can climb / sing / see / run / fly*. Now ask *Can a cat fly? Can a bird shout? Can a cat sing? Can a bird climb?* When the children say *No*, get them to expand this to *No, it can't*. You could then ask about other animals (e.g. a dog, a mouse, a cow, a horse).

STUDENT'S BOOK

 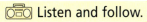 **10 minutes**

Refresh the children's memory of the last episode of the story.
- *With the mother tongue:* Ask what they can remember from last time.
- *Without the mother tongue:* On the board, draw a simple picture of a balloon with four people and a dog in the basket. Ask *Who's this?* and elicit the names of the characters. Draw some birds nearby. Ask *What's this?* and *What's the problem?* Say and mime *RRRIPPP!*

LISTENING TO THE STORY Play the recording through and ask the children to look at the pictures. Then play it again and pause after pictures 1 and 2. Ask the children *Where are they? (In a tree.) What can they do? (They can jump.) Look at Kip. What's the problem? (He can't jump.)*

Play the recording for pictures 3 and 4. Say *Look at Kip. What's the problem now? (He can't walk.)*

Play the recording for pictures 5 and 6. You could ask *Is Tom a good boy?* The children might answer *Yes, he can help the children* or *No, his Mom and Dad are cold.* Finally, play the whole recording through again.

ACTING OUT Divide the class into pairs or small groups and get the children to read the dialog.

Then ask some children to act out the story (six parts: Jess, Nick, Tom, Kip, and Tom's parents). They can read from their books, or you could supply prompts:

1 What can we do?   2 I can't jump!   3 I can't walk!   4 Silly Kip!   5 Tom!   6 Let's go!

As before, you could use a large box as a balloon basket. You could also cover the parents with a blanket which Tom pulls off.

Classroom language and answer key

Open your books to page 40. Look at the pictures. Listen.

Work in pairs/groups. Read the words.

Let's act out the story. Who wants to be Jess? Who wants to be Nick? Very good!

4C • I can help.

Look at the picture.
Find a horse. Find a …

What animal is this?
Show me in the picture.

Answers
1 a cow   2 a hen   3 a dog
4 a cat   5 a horse   6 a chick
7 a duck

Answers
can fly: duck
can swim: horse, cow, duck, dog
can run fast: horse, cow
can climb: cat
can jump high: dog, cat, horse
can't fly: chick, hen, cow, horse, dog, cat
can't jump high: cow, duck, hen, chick
can't swim: hen, chick

Answers
2 Cows can't climb.
3 Chicks can't swim.
4 Dogs can't fly.
5 Cats can't read.
6 Horses can't talk.

2   Look at Tom's farm. Match the animals and the words.   10 minutes

Read through the names of the animals with the children and introduce *duck*, *hen*, and *chick*. Then you could do one of the following:

- Imitate the sound that each animal makes as you say its name. Ask the children to find each animal in the picture.
- Make the sound without naming the animal. The children point at the animal in the picture and say *Here it is*. Ask *What is it?* and help them to say the name of the animal.

EXTRA IDEAS

- You could say the name of the animal and all the children have to make the sound.
- You could divide the class up into groups of "cows," "horses," "ducks," etc. When you call out the name of the animal, the children in that group have to make their sound.

3   Listen. What animal can you hear?   10 minutes

Play the recording and pause after each sound. The children have to say what animal it is.

4   Look at the picture in Exercise 2. Think. Find an animal that …   10 minutes

Ask the children to work with their neighbor. They need to look at the picture in Exercise 2 and find an animal for each phrase. (There are usually several animals that they could choose.)

EXTRA IDEA   The children each think of an animal. Then individuals mime what their animal can do and the rest of the class try to guess what animal it is.

Further practice: Activity Book Exercises 1 and 2.

ACTIVITY BOOK

1   Think. What's wrong? Write sentences.   10 minutes

New language: talk

Ask the children what they can say about the picture before they write their answers. You could put the verbs on the board.

2   Play a game. Use your spinner. Color the board.   10 minutes

Note: This exercise needs to be done in class. The children need their spinners.

The exercise reviews language in the form of a game, using the spinners that the children made in *Welcome!* C (see teaching notes on the Activity Book on page T9). When they spin their spinner and land on a number, they have to answer a question about animals, say a number, or make a sentence with *can/can't*. Before or after playing the game, they can color in the pictures.

2 Look at Tom's farm. Match the animals and the words.

a horse   a cow   a duck   a hen   a chick   a dog   a cat

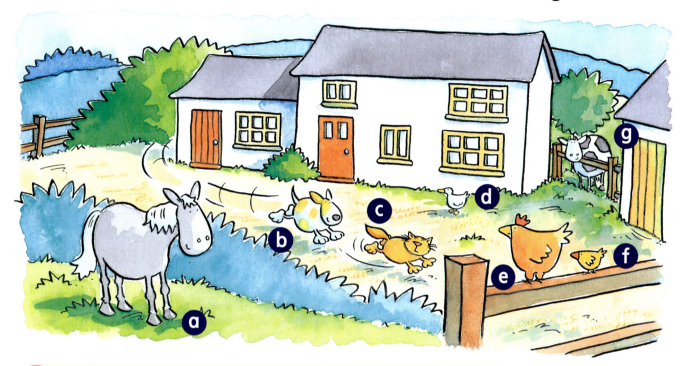

3 🔊 Listen. What animal can you hear?

4 Look at the picture in Exercise 2. Think. Find an animal that …

can fly   can swim   can run fast   can climb

can jump high   can't fly   can't jump high   can't swim

4D Taffy the dog

1 Listen and follow.

4D • Storytime: Taffy the dog

Topic
Taffy is a smart dog. He gets a man and his daughter to take him for a walk, but it starts raining and Taffy decides he doesn't want to leave the car. The father tells his daughter to walk with Taffy while he drives the car. Taffy then bites the tire. The father has to find a telephone – and Taffy and the girl get back in the car!

Aims
- To develop the children's listening and speaking fluency.
- To review language presented in earlier units.

Language
Review
Come on!
We can't walk now
Where's my …
I can …, you can …

New language
Stop it!
Get out!
Thank you.
Go away.
rain, umbrella, smart, telephone, go out, drive, stay here

What you need
- CD and player.
- Cut-out 7 (Teacher's Book, page T123) for Exercise 2.
- Posterboard, scissors, glue, string, markers, and tape for Exercise 2.
- Optional: a ready-made Taffy mask for Exercise 2.
- An umbrella for Exercise 3.

Before you begin
You could start by making the Taffy mask in Exercise 2 first. This will stimulate the children's interest in the story.

STUDENT'S BOOK

1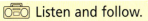

You can start by telling the story while the children look at the pictures. Point to the pictures and slowly say what is happening. If you add some new words you can provide a richer context for the children to try to understand – they do not need to understand every word. For example:

1. *Look. There's a man. There's a girl. And here's a dog. His name's Taffy. Taffy is a smart dog.*
2. *Taffy wants to walk. He wants to go out.*
3. *Oh no! Look! It's raining. The man says, "Rain! We can't walk now."*
4. *The man looks for his umbrella. Taffy is here.*
5. *The man says, "I can drive and you can walk with Taffy." The girl says, "Oh, thank you, Dad!"*
6. *Look! Look at Taffy! Bang! Hissss!*
7. *What can they do?*
8. *And now the man must walk to the telephone in the rain! Taffy and the girl can stay in the car.*

Play the recording once or twice while the children follow the story in their books. Then divide the class into pairs to read the dialog.

Classroom language and answer key

Open your books.
Let me tell you a story.
Listen. Look at this picture.

Listen. Follow the story.
Work together.
Read the story.

4D • Taffy the dog

Cut the mask. Carefully!
Color the mask.
Make a hole here and here.
Put the string in here.
Put the tape here.
Like this.
Put it on!

Who wants to act out the story?
You are the man. You are the girl.

Answers
11, eleven; 12, twelve;
8, eight; 15, fifteen;
14, fourteen; 16, sixteen;
20, twenty

Example answers
Birds can fly and jump.
Birds can't swim.
Bears can swim.
Bears can't jump or fly.
Dogs can jump and swim.
Dogs can't fly.
Cats can jump.
Cats can't swim or fly.

Answers
bird, fly; mouse, fly; mouse, run, climb; bird, mouse

2 Make a Taffy mask.   20+ minutes

Use Cut-out 7, page T123 in the Teacher's Book.

It is a good idea to show the children a completed Taffy mask before they begin. Make sure that each child has a copy of Cut-out 7.

You may want to prepare some of the materials beforehand. Making the holes for the strings is particularly tricky. Some questions to consider:

- Should the children cut out the mask, or should you?
- Should the children color the mask at home or in class?
- Should the children make the holes for the strings, or should you?
- Should the children reinforce the holes with tape, or should you?
- Should the children tie on the strings, or should you?

3 Act out the story. Use your Taffy mask.   10 minutes

You can now ask some children to act out the story (three parts: the man, his daughter, and Taffy). To help them, you could put the dialog on the board.

ACTIVITY BOOK Review

1 Draw lines.   10 minutes

It is a good idea to read through the numbers with the children and get them to do the sums before they match them to the answers.

2 Draw —— to show what they can do.
Draw ～～ to show what they can't do.   10 minutes

Explain to the children what they have to do. You will get differences of opinion, as it depends on how they see *fly*, *swim*, and *jump high*. For example, some birds can fly, some can swim, and some can jump high.

3 Read the poem. Write the words.   10 minutes

New language: cry, happy

This poem is intended to be read aloud. Go through it with the children. You could ask them to write down the missing words.

I can …   5 minutes

Before they color in the stars, go through the examples with the children. Get them to count to 20, and to say what they can and can't do.

Picture Dictionary 4

The children can now complete Picture Dictionary 4 on page 45.

EXTRA PRACTICE Optional work is on pages T96 and T97 in the Teacher's Book.

Answers
1 2 chick   3 duck   4 cat   5 bear   6 horse   7 hen   8 bird   9 dog
2 eleven, 12, fourteen, 15, seventeen, nineteen, twenty
   eighteen, nineteen, thirteen, seventeen, twenty, thirteen
3 Australia, red, jump
4 This is a tiger. Tigers come from Asia. They are yellow/orange and black. Tigers can climb.
   This is a zebra. Zebras come from Africa. They are black and white. Zebras can run very fast.

❸ Rain! We can't walk now.

Get out, Taffy!

Oh, thank you, Dad!

❽ There's a telephone. You can walk and I can stay here with Taffy!

Grrr!

2 Make a Taffy mask.

You need:

cut-out 7   scissors   string
markers   tape   card   glue

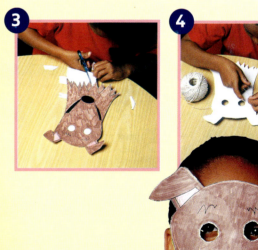

3 Act out the story. Use your Taffy mask.

43

Review

1 Think. Find five strange things.

The cat is ...

2 What can you do? What can't you do?

sing

run very fast

fly

jump very high

climb a tree

3 Talk about a friend.

My friend, Dan, can't sing.

4 Play the game with your spinner.

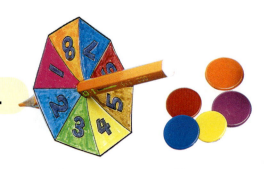

Review

Topic
This section contains review exercises and a board game.

Aim
- To review the language covered in Units 3 and 4.

Language
colors
can, can't

What you need
- CD and player.
- The children need their spinners for Exercise 4.

STUDENT'S BOOK

1 Think. Find five strange things. 10 minutes

Give the children some time to work in pairs to choose the five things that are wrong, and to decide what they can say. Then ask for their answers. You could also ask them to write down their answers.

2 What can you do? What can't you do? 5 minutes

Using the verbs given, ask some children *Can you sing? Can you fly?* Encourage complete answers: *Yes, I can. No, I can't.*

The children can then work in pairs and ask each other. Go around the class, helping as necessary. This step prepares the children for Exercise 3.

3 Talk about a friend. 5 minutes

Now ask some children to tell the class about the person they worked with.

Classroom language and answer key

Answers
The cat is blue.
The horse is green.
The banana is red.
The cow is blue.
The mouse is red.

Ask your friend.

Tell me two things he/she can do / can't do.

T44

Review

4 **Play the game with your spinner.** 20+ minutes

For this game, the children will need the spinners that they made in *Welcome!* C (see teaching notes on the Activity Book on page T9). They will each need a game piece or a coin to show where they are on the board.

The game works in the same way as the game in Unit 2 *Review*. Divide the class into pairs or threes and explain how to play.

1 Everyone puts their game pieces on *Start*.
2 The players take turns spinning their spinners and moving the game pieces forward according to the number they get when it lands. They should say this number and count their moves forward aloud.
3 When they land on a tile, they have to follow an instruction or answer a question. If they can't do it, the others in the group can help (there is no penalty for not knowing the answer).
4 The tiles with arrows mean "Go forward" or "Go back" the number of tiles shown on the arrow.
5 To finish, a player must land on *Finish* with the exact number. If the spinner shows a number that is too big to finish, the player counts into *Finish* and back out again.

5 Hello, Ben!

5A Sharks!

1 🔊 Listen and follow.

1 Look, Tom. We have a map.
Wow! Where are we?

2 I think we're here.
I have a telescope. Let's see.

3 Yes! I can see an island and ... aaah! There are sharks!
WHAT!

4 Don't worry! We're safe up here.

5 SPLASH!

6 Look, a shark!

Act it out!

5A • Sharks!

Topic
The children are now over the sea in their balloon. Tom has a telescope and he sees an island and … sharks! The children think they are safe in the balloon when suddenly a tsunami, a giant wave, hits the balloon.

Aim
- To teach the meaning and use of *have*.

Language
I have/ You have/ We have
I think we're here.
Let's see.
Don't worry.
They can …
telescope, island, shark, ship, sea, fish

What you need
- CD and player.
- Optional: a bag containing various objects for "Before you begin."
- Optional: a box and a cardboard roll for Exercise 1.
- Optional: "paper bangers" (see *Extra activities*, page T83 in the Teacher's Book) for Exercise 1.

Before you begin
You could start by teaching the use of *I have/You have/We have*, using one or more of these approaches:
- Bring in some things in a bag and show the children what you have. Take the things out slowly one by one and talk about them: *What do I have in my bag? Let's see. I have a pen. I have a sweet. I have a map*, etc.
- Ask the children to say what they have. Encourage complete sentences: *I have …*
- Talk about the things in the classroom: *What do we have in our classroom? We have a map on the wall. We have a picture on the door*, etc.

STUDENT'S BOOK

**** **Listen and follow.**   20+ minutes

Ask questions about the story so far, either in English or in the mother tongue.

LISTENING TO THE STORY Ask the children to close their books, unless you think they would find it too difficult. Play the recording and pause after pictures 1 and 2. Ask *Where are they?* (*They're in the balloon.*) *What do they have?* (*They have a map.*) *Tom says "I have …" what?* Answer the question yourself: *A telescope. He says "I have a telescope,"* and mime looking through a telescope.

Play the recording for pictures 3 and 4. Ask *What can Tom see?* (*He can see an island and sharks.*) Draw a picture of a shark on the board, and show an expression of panic. Continue: *Zara says "Don't worry." It's OK. Why?* (*They are up high.*) Show relief.

Say *But …* and play the recording for the last two pictures. Ask the children to open their books. Point out the wave in picture 4 and say *Look at the sea.* You could teach *wave* and say *There's a very big wave. SPLASH!* Play the recording through twice. The children listen with their books open.

ACTING OUT First, divide the class into pairs and get them to read the dialog. Then ask some children to act out the story (six parts: Jess, Nick, Joanne, Zara, Tom, and a silent Kip). You could supply prompts on the board:

*1 We have a map. Where …?   2 I think … a telescope.   3 I can see …
4 Don't worry.   5 Splash!   6 A shark!*

As before, the children could stand in a box simulating the balloon basket. Tom could use a cardboard roll as a telescope. If the children have made paper bangers (see *Extra activities*, page T83 in the Teacher's Book), they can be used to dramatize the wave crashing into the balloon.

Further practice: Activity Book Exercise 1.

Classroom language and answer key

*Close your books.
Listen.
Where are they?
What do they have?*

What can Tom see?

Open your books at page 46. Listen and follow in your books.

*Work in pairs.
Read the words.*

*I need six children.
Who wants to act out the story?
Come to the front of the class.*

5A • Sharks!

What's your number?

Answers
2 You have a ball.
3 You have a telescope.
4 You have a fish.
5 You have a bag.
6 You have a shark

*Let's read the words first.
Listen and sing!
Do the actions.*

Answer
Sentence: I can see three sharks.

Answers
ruler: No   map: Yes
ball: Yes   pen: Yes
sandwich: No   pencil: Yes
book: Yes   telescope: Yes
pencil case: No   bag: Yes

---

2 Ask your friends for a number. Say what they have. 12 minutes

You can start by saying *Let's go fishing! Look at the picture. What's in the water?* Elicit the names: *a telescope, a fish, two sharks, a bag, a ball*.

Ask a child to choose a number, 1–6. Ask *What's your number?* Follow the line with your finger and tell them what they have. Then choose some numbers yourself. Get different children to ask *What's your number?* and to tell you what you have. Insist on full sentences: *You have …*

Now put the children into groups to ask each other. Go around the class, encouraging the children to produce full, correct sentences.

Further practice: Activity Book Exercises 2 and 3.

3 Sing a song. 10 minutes

Read through the words with the children first. Then play the recording and get them to sing along. You could get them to make actions with their hands for *ships, fish, sharks, see,* and *eat*.

ACTIVITY BOOK

1 Find the way. 10 minutes

The children have to find their way to the ship, collecting words as they go. They then draw what Carolina can see in the telescope.

2 What do Benny and Carolina have? Write *Yes* or *No*. 10 minutes

The children have to read the sentences, look carefully at the picture and write *Yes* or *No*.

3 Draw four things in your bag. Write the words. 10 minutes

The children can draw anything they wish in the bag. Ask them to suggest some things in English. To remind them of other words they have learned, you could make a selection of Vocabulary Cards from Units 1–4. As you hold up each one, the children say what it is. You could then get the class to help you spell some of the words on the board.

2 Ask your friends for a number. Say what they have.

Number 1.   You have a shark.

3 🎵 Sing a song.

There are ships, ships, ships in the sea,
In the sea, in the sea.
There are ships, ships, ships in the sea,
And they can see me.

There are fish, fish, fish in the sea,
And they can see me.

There are sharks, sharks, sharks in the sea,
But they can eat me!
Aaaaaah! It's a shark!

5B King Cat's corner

1 Chant with me!

Pat your head and pull your ear,

Pat your nose and pull it here!

Open your mouth, close one eye,

Pull your hair, and say goodbye!

2 Say and write the colors.

a ..brown.. eyes   b .... eyes   c   .... eyes

d .... hair   e   .... hair   f   ..red.. hair

g   ..long.. hair   h ....short.. hair   i ..blond.. hair

3 Describe your hair and eyes.   I have ...

5B • King Cat's corner

Topic
King Cat presents puzzles and exercises.

Aims
- To teach the names of parts of the head and face, and types of hair.
- To teach *He has* and *She has*.

Language
head, ear, nose, mouth, eye, hair
long, short, blond
pat, pull, close, say
He has … She has …

What you need
- CD and player.

Before you begin

- You could play "Simon says" (see *Extra activities*, page T81 in the Teacher's Book). Instruct the children to do some actions. If you don't say *Simon says*, the children shouldn't do the action. Actions: *Stand up, Sit down, Hop, Jump, Clap*.
- You could say *Let's learn some new words*. Give the following instructions and do the actions. The children can copy you. *Pat your head. Pat your nose. Open your mouth. Close one eye. Pull your hair. Say goodbye. Pat your mouth. Pull your nose. Close two eyes.*

STUDENT'S BOOK

1 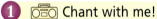 **10 minutes**

If you have used the ideas in "Before you begin," the children will find this easy. The emphasis is on getting them to chant the words as they do the actions.
Further practice: Activity Book Exercise 1.

2 Say and write the colors. **10 minutes**

The children can work in pairs to decide what the colors are. You can then go through their answers before they write. It is a good idea to write the missing words on the board so that they spell them correctly in their books. Alternatively, they can write them in their notebooks.

3 Describe your hair and eyes. **5 minutes**

Point to pictures g, h, and i, and say *Look. She/He has long/short/blond hair*. Point out examples of children in the class, if possible. You could ask *Does (name) have long/short/blond hair?* (but don't teach the question form here).

Ask different children *What color hair/eyes do you have?* Some children won't know what color their eyes are, so you could ask their neighbor to tell them. This will allow you to naturally use *He/She has*, but don't teach this form yet. Get each child to say two correct sentences about their hair and eyes.

Classroom language and answer key

Do the actions with me.
Let's do it again.
Listen and chant with King Cat.

What color are they?
What color is it?

Answers
b blue   c green   d brown
e black

Tell me about your hair and eyes.
Look at …'s eyes.
What color are they?

Tell me about (name).
What color hair does he/she have?
What color eyes does he/she have?

5B • King Cat's corner

Read the sentences.
Match them to the pictures.

Answers
a Bill b Bill c Alice d Bill
e Alice f Alice

4 🔊 Match the sentences and the pictures. **10 minutes**

Allow the children a few minutes to work together and read through the sentences. They must then decide if each sentence is about the boy or the girl. Play the recording, and stop it after each sentence to check their answers.

EXTRA IDEA You could encourage the children to produce sentences with two adjectives – that is, *big/small, long/short* and the colors. For example: *He has short brown hair. She has big green eyes.* Ask them to describe people in the class in this way. To help them, you can put some key words on the board:

  He has …   She has …
   long short   big small
         hair   eyes

You could give a few "nonsense" examples and ask if they sound right, for example, *He has short green eyes.*

Further practice: Activity Book Exercises 2 and 3.

5 Play a game. Choose a picture and tell your friend. **10 minutes**

To show the children how the game works, choose one of the pictures and describe it in one sentence, for example, *She has short hair.* (picture 2). Ask a pair of children which picture it is. The other children in the class can help them.

If the pair can't give the correct answer, put a mark on the board. Give another piece of information about the same picture, for example, *She has a small mouth.* If they still don't guess correctly, put another mark on the board. Continue until they have the correct answer.

Then reverse roles. Ask the pair to choose a picture and to describe it. You can then guess. If you are wrong, put a mark on the board. When you have guessed, count up the marks. The winners are the players with the fewest marks.

Now divide the class into pairs to play the game. They will need a pencil to keep a record of their marks. They can play two or three times.

Further practice: Activity Book Exercise 4.

ACTIVITY BOOK

1 Write the words.

The children look at the clues and write the words in the puzzle.

Work in pairs.
Choose a picture.
Tell your friend one piece of information.
Guess. Which picture is it?.

Answers
2 mouse 3 nose 4 red
5 big 6 eyes 7 ears

2 Write the names.

The children read each sentence and decide who it is about.

Answers
big eyes: Suzy
long hair: Tim
small eyes: Bella
short hair: Nino

3 This is my friend, Bill. Draw his face.

The children read the sentences and draw Bill's face.

4 Draw a face. Color it. Ask your friend to describe it.

The children can complete their drawing at home. Then allow some time in the next class for pairs to show their drawings and describe each other's.

4 Match the sentences and the pictures.

a) He has blue eyes.
b) He has short hair.
c) She has green eyes.
d) He has a big mouth.
e) She has long hair.
f) She has a small mouth.

Alice

Bill

 5 Play a game. Choose a picture and tell your friend.

He has ...   She has ...

1) Sam

2) Clara

3) Mike

4) Carol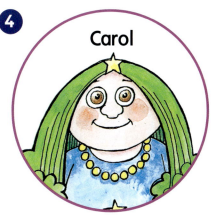

5) Helen

6) Ted

5C Thanks, Ben.

1 🔊 Listen and follow.

Act it out!

5C • Thanks, Ben.

Topic
Jess, Joanne, Tom, Zara, and Nick are in the sea. There are sharks in the sea. Nick thinks a shark has him but he is saved by someone in a boat. It is Ben. Ben lives in a tree house with a monkey, Mickey. Ben knows what the strange symbol on the map is …

Aims
- To introduce the children to the present simple (positive form).

Language
Sharks eat people.
They eat …
Oh no! A shark!
Don't worry.
Who are you?
We live in a tree house.
I know what that is.
I see it every day.
They live/eat …
monkey, crocodile, tiger,
in rivers, in forests, in the sea,
on farms, fruit, grass

What you need
- CD and player.

Before you begin

Before you start, you could teach the meaning and use of *live* and *eat*. Ask the children if they can remember what happened in the last part of the story: *Where are the children?* (*In the sea.*) *Where's the balloon?* (*In the sea.*) *What can Nick see?* (*A shark.*)

You can continue: *That's right. Sharks live in the sea. Are big sharks dangerous?* (*Yes, they are.*) *Why?* Help the children answer *They can eat people!* Ask *What other animals live in the sea?* Elicit the word *fish* (the children might also want to use other words, like *octopus* or *whale*). Say *That's right. Big sharks eat fish – and they can eat people!*

STUDENT'S BOOK

 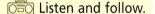

LISTENING TO THE STORY The children can have their books open or closed as you and they prefer. Play the recording but stop it after every two pictures and ask some questions:

- Pictures 1 and 2: *Kip isn't happy. Why?* (*Sharks eat dogs!*) *Nick says, "Oh no!" Why?* (*There's a shark.*) *That's terrible!*
- Pictures 3 and 4: *Does a shark have Nick?* (*No.*) *Who is in a boat?* (*Ben.*) *Who lives with Ben?* (*Mickey, his monkey.*)
- Pictures 5 and 6: *Ben and Mickey live … where?* (*In a tree house.*) *Joanne says, "Ben, what's this?" What does Joanne have?* (*The map.*)

Play the recording all the way through once or twice.

ACTING OUT Divide the class into pairs or small groups and get them to read out the dialog.

Ask some children to act out the story (seven parts: Jess, Nick, Tom, Zara, Joanne, Ben, and Kip). They can read from their books, you could write the dialog on the board, or you could supply prompts:

1 Help! Sharks eat … They eat …   2 Oh no! …
3 Don't worry. Thank you. But …   4 I'm Ben. And that's …   5 We live in a …
6 What's this? I know … I see it …

You could arrange chairs to make Ben's boat and a table in his tree house that the children can sit around.

> *Classroom language and answer key*

> *I need seven children.*
> *Who wants to be Jess?*
> *Who wants to be Nick?*

5C • Thanks, Ben.

Answers
Horses live on farms. They eat grass. Crocodiles live in rivers. They eat animals. Monkeys live in forests. They eat fruit. Tigers live in forests. They eat animals.

Look at the pictures in Exercise 2 again. Talk about an animal. Guess!

Answers
```
s f g j n q e s t d
t f o r e s t e n m
m o n k e y n k o t
u g e h b s h a r k
j k f l s h w l e h
r e t w s e a d w k
c r o c o d i l e p
f j k l j k b d j g
t i g e r b p o e r
g r i v e r h w w e
```
(forest, monkey, shark, sea, crocodile, tiger, river circled)

Answers
b 7 tigers   c 6 sharks
d 5 monkeys

Answers
Frogs live in rivers. They eat insects.
Foxes live in forests. They eat hens/chicks/animals.

Answers
tree, monkey, hear, birds, tree see, tigers, happy, forest see, sharks, sea, happy

---

2 Think. Match the animals, places, and the foods. Tell the class.   15 minutes

Introduce the exercise with some questions: *Sharks live ... where?* (*In the sea.*) *Yes, that's right! What about crocodiles? Crocodiles live ... where?* (*In rivers.*) *Sharks eat ... what?* (*Fish.*) *What about crocodiles? Crocodiles eat ...* (*Animals.*)

Now the children open their books. Read through the names of the animals, places and types of food with them. Give them a few minutes to match each animal with the place and the food. Point out that we say **on farms**, not *in*.

Further practice: Activity Book Exercise 1.

3 Talk about an animal. Your friend can guess.   10 minutes

Demonstrate by giving some information about one of the animals in Exercise 2. For example: *They live in the sea. Guess! They eat fruit. Guess!* Get the children to guess the animal.

Divide the class into pairs so they can work in the same way. To help, you can put some prompts on the board: *They live in/on ... They eat ...*

EXTRA IDEA You could write the names of some other animals on the board and ask the children where they live and what they eat. Give them any new words that they need to express their ideas (e.g. *meat, seeds*).

Cats   (They live in houses. They eat meat.)
Bears   (They live in forests. They eat fruit.)
Chickens   (They live on farms. They eat seeds.)
Cows   (They live on farms. They eat grass.)
Dogs   (They live in houses. They eat meat.)

Further practice: Activity Book Exercises 2, 3, and 4.

ACTIVITY BOOK

1 Find six more words. Draw lines.   10 minutes

Check that the children know the name of each animal before they look for and circle the words in the puzzle.

2 Read the sentences. Write the animals and the numbers from Exercise 1.   10 minutes

New language: insects
The children write the names of the animals and write the number from Exercise 1.

3 Write about some animals.   10 minutes

New language: frogs, foxes, insects
Before the children write, ask them what they can say. Note that *frogs* and *foxes* are new words, and they will need *insects* to describe what frogs eat.

4 Read Ben's poem. Write the words.   10 minutes

New language: happy, free, zoo
First, look at the large picture with the children, as this will help them understand the poem. Ask them questions about what they can see.

Read through the poem with the children and get them to figure out the missing words. They can write these in later.

2 Think. Match the animals, the places, and the foods. Tell the class.

Sharks live in the sea. They eat fish.

sharks   horses   crocodiles   monkeys   tigers

in rivers   in forests   in the sea   on farms

animals   fruit   fish   grass

3 Talk about an animal. Your friend can guess.

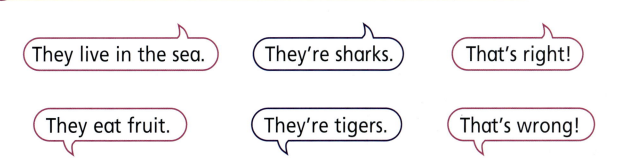

They live in the sea.   They're sharks.   That's right!

They eat fruit.   They're tigers.   That's wrong!

5D The smart fish

1 🔊 Listen and follow.

5D • Storytime: The smart fish

Topic
A small fish is swimming in the sea. Suddenly, a shark appears. He is about to eat the fish, when the fish tells the shark that his brother is much bigger – and that his brother can eat the shark. The shark doesn't believe this – but the fish proves him wrong!

Aims
- To develop the children's listening and speaking fluency.
- To review language covered in earlier units.

Language
Review
can, can't
You can't …
Yes, I can.
No, you can't.
present simple: eat
have

New language
Where is he?
Who's that?
brother, catch, card

What you need
- CD and player.
- Optional: Cut-out 8 (Teacher's Book, page T124) for Exercise 2.
- Posterboard, glue, scissors, tape, string, and markers for Exercise 2.
- Optional: a ready-made "shark snapper" for Exercise 2.

Before you begin

As before, you could change the order of the exercises and get the children to make their shark snapper before they listen to the story.

STUDENT'S BOOK

You can start by telling the story while the children look at the pictures. Point to the pictures and slowly say what is happening. For example:
1 Look. There are fish in the sea. They are swimming away fast. But look at this fish. He isn't swimming.
2 Suddenly, a shark comes! He wants to eat the fish. The fish says, "Stop! You can't eat me!" The shark says he can. "I'm a shark," he says.
3 "No, no," says the fish. The shark says, "I'm a shark. I eat everything." Oh!
4 The fish has an idea. He's a smart fish. He says, "You can't eat me!" He says, "I have a BIG brother and he can eat YOU!" The shark says, "Oh yes? Where?"
5 The fish swims away – fast. "You can't catch me," he says.
6 The shark can't find the fish.
7 The shark sees a cave. Look! He hears a voice. "Stop!" it says.
8 The voice says, "You can't eat my brother. I can eat you." The shark is frightened. "Help!" he says.
9 The shark goes away fast!

Play the recording once or twice while the children follow the story in their books. Then divide the class into pairs to read the dialog.

Classroom language and answer key

Let me tell you a story.
Look at the pictures.
Look at picture 1 …

Listen and follow.
Work in pairs.
Read the words.

5D • The smart fish

Draw a box.
Cut the posterboard.
Draw a fish. Cut the posterboard.

Stick the fish on the posterboard.
Follow me.
Put the string here.
Use the tape.
Play with your shark!

Who wants to act out the story?
You are the fish. You are the shark.

Answers
2 head 3 hair 4 ear
5 monkey 6 forest

Answers
big ears, blue eyes, red nose, long hair, big mouth.

Answers
It's a crocodile.

2 Make a shark snapper.   10 minutes

Optional: use Cut-out 8, page T124 in the Teacher's Book.

It is a good idea to show the children a completed shark snapper before they begin. Make sure that each child has all the materials that they need. If you use Cut-out 8, the children will need some glue to paste the cut-out onto the posterboard.

This activity requires careful control of scissors and tape. If the children are going to use scissors, make sure they use safe children's scissors. You may want to prepare some materials beforehand. Some questions to consider:

- Should the children draw and cut the posterboard themselves (for the shark and the fish) and decorate it, or should you use Cut-out 8?
- Should the children attach the string, or should you?

3 Act out the story. Use your shark snapper.   10 minutes

You can now ask some children to act out the story. You will need a "fish" and a "shark." The "shark" can use the shark snapper when he/she is chasing after the fish. You can put prompts or the complete text on the board.

ACTIVITY BOOK Review

1 Write the words.   10 minutes

Go through the names of the things or animals in the pictures.

2 Find the way. Draw the man. Write what he has.   15 minutes

The children have to find the correct route to the face and "collect" words along the way. The words tell them what to draw.

3 Read, think, and draw.   15 minutes

The children have to read, draw the animal, and then write its name.

I can …   5 minutes

Before the children color in the stars, go through some examples. Get them to say what they have in their bag or on their desk, to describe a friend's face, and to say what different animals eat and where they live.

Picture Dictionary 5

The children can now complete Picture Dictionary 5 on page 62.

EXTRA PRACTICE There are optional *Extra practice* exercises for this unit on pages T98 and T99 in the Teacher's Book. Note: For Exercise 4 the children will need to find extra information about pandas and hippos.

Answers
1 eye, nose, hair, ear, mouth
2 **Dog:** It has long hair and big ears. **Cat:** It has short hair and big eyes.
  Bird: It has small eyes and a small mouth. **Elephant:** It has big ears and small eyes.
  Horse: It has a long nose and big eyes.
3 **Daniel:** He has a bag. **Steve:** He has a ball. **Nadia:** She has a book.
  Sue: She has a tree. **Maria and Sam:** They have a shark.
4 Pandas live in China. They eat plants. Hippos live in Africa. They eat plants.

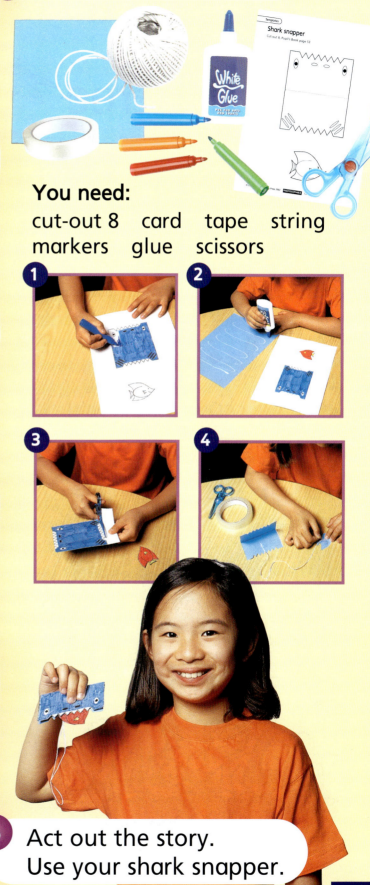

6 Goodbye!

6A The tree

1 🎧 Listen and follow.

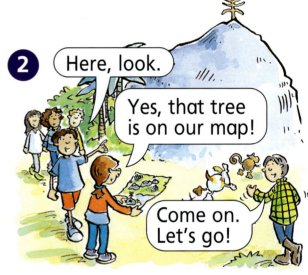

Act it out!

6A • The tree

Topic
The children are near the end of their journey. Ben shows them the meaning of the shape on the map. It's a tree – but why is it on the map? They climb a hill to get closer to the tree, but Tom falls off the cliff. Mickey and Kip race after him.

Aims
- To introduce the present simple question form (receptive ability only).
- To teach short answers: *Yes, I do / No, I don't.*

Language
Do you like …?
Yes, I do. No, I don't.
I like it/them, too.
Follow me!
Here we are.
Why is it …?
Are you OK? I'm OK.
Let me think.
ice cream, fish, milk, cheese, apples, oranges, pears

What you need
- CD and player.
- Optional: a large piece of paper (for a "map") in Exercise 1.

Before you begin

You could start by introducing *Do you like …?* as a fixed phrase. Ask some children about their favorite things. For example, you could ask *What's your favorite color?* and then *Do you like black? Do you like green?* Ask a few children around the class.

Then ask *What's your favorite fruit?* and *Do you like …?* with the fruit in Exercise 2. Ask about other food in Exercise 2 (ice cream, fish, milk, cheese). Once you are sure that the children understand *Do you like …?* encourage them to reply with *Yes, I do* or *No, I don't.*

STUDENT'S BOOK

1 **Listen and follow.**   10 minutes

Refresh the children's memory of the story. Ask some questions, for example, *Where are the children?* (*On an island.*) *Who lives there?* (*Ben.*) *Where is Ben's house?* (*In a tree.*) *Who is Ben's friend?* (*Mickey the monkey.*) On the board, draw the shape of the symbol near the X on the map, and ask *Where's this?* (*On the map.*)

LISTENING TO THE STORY The children can have their books open or closed as you and they prefer. Play the recording through. Point to your drawing of the symbol on the board and ask *What is the thing on the map?* (*A tree.*) *Ben says, "Follow me!" Where to?* (*To the tree.*) Then ask *Where is Tom?* If the children have their books open, they can point and answer *He's here.* If their books are closed, they can answer *I don't know.*

Play the recording in sections. Suggested questions:
- Pictures 1 and 2: *Ben asks, "Do you like coconuts?" What does Zara say? What does Kip say? Why is the tree important?* (*It's on the map.*)
- Pictures 3 and 4: *Ben says, "Follow me!" Where to?* (*The tree.*) *Where are they now?* (*Near the tree.*)
- Pictures 5 and 6: *Is Tom OK?* (*Yes.*) *Where is he?* (*Here.*) *What can they do now?* (*They can yell for help. They can climb down. Tom can climb up.*)

ACTING OUT Divide the class into pairs or groups to read the dialog.

Then ask some children to act out the story (eight parts: Jess, Nick, Joanne, Zara, Ben, Tom, Kip, and Mickey). Suggested prompts:

1 Coconuts?   2 That tree is …   3 Follow me!   4 Why is it on our map? Mickey …!
5 OK?   6 What can we do now? Mickey! Kip!

The children could use a large piece of paper as their map.

Classroom language and answer key

Can you remember the story?

Open/Close your books.
Listen.

Listen again.

Work in pairs.
Read the words.

I need six children! Who wants to act out the story? Who wants to be Jess? (etc.)

T54

6A • The tree

Work in pairs.
Ask your neighbor.

Let's sing a song.
Let's read the words first.
Listen and sing!

Answers
2 cheese   3 an orange
4 ice cream   5 a banana
6 milk   7 an apple
8 a pear

Answers
I eat fruit. I drink milk. I play a sport. I watch TV. I talk on the telephone.

2 Ask your friend.   10 minutes

You can use Vocabulary Cards 26 and 82–88 to teach or review the food words. If you have not already introduced *Do you like …?*, you should do that now. Divide the class into pairs to ask and answer.

Further practice: Activity Book Exercises 1 and 2.

3 Sing a song.   10 minutes

Read through the words with the children first. Then play the recording and get them to sing along.

When they are confident in singing the song, choose a different child to answer each time. You could also change *fish* and *apples* to other things from Exercise 2.

Point out to the class that we say *it* for single things – all the things in the first line in Exercise 2 – and *them* for more than one (all the things in the second line).

Further practice: Activity Book Exercises 3 and 4.

ACTIVITY BOOK

1 Find seven more things. Draw lines and write the words.   15 minutes

The children have to look carefully at the picture to find the things. They may not produce the article *a* or *an*, but you can supply it as you confirm their answers.

2 Write your answers.   15 minutes

Read through the questions with the children. They then write *Yes, I do* or *No, I don't* or *I don't know* for each.

**3 What do you do every day? Check the boxes.
What does Steve say? Check the boxes.   20 minutes**

New language: go to school, drink, play on a computer, play a sport, go swimming, talk to, talk on the telephone, watch TV

Read through the sentences with the children. They read them again and check the boxes labeled *Me*.

The children then look at the thought bubbles and check the boxes labeled *Steve*.

2 Ask your friend. (Do you like ... ?) (Yes, I do.) (No, I don't.)

ice cream   fish   milk   cheese

bananas   apples   oranges   pears

3  Sing a song.

I like fish, I like fish.
Daniel, do you like it, too?

Oh, I don't know.
Let me think.
Yes, I do. I like it, too!

I like apples, I like apples.
Tina, do you like them, too?

Oh, I don't know.
Let me think.
Yes, I do. I like them, too!

6B King Cat's corner

1 Tell your friend about your day.

> I go to school by bus. I go home by car. After school, I play soccer.

I go to school ...
I go home ...

by bus   by car   by bike   on foot

After school,

I do my homework   I play soccer   I watch TV

2  Chant with me!

Monday, Tuesday,
Monday, Tuesday,
Two days of the week
Two days of the week
But what's next?
Wednesday!

Monday, Tuesday, Wednesday,
Monday, Tuesday, Wednesday,
Three days of the week
Three days of the week
But what's next?
Thursday!

Friday   Saturday   Sunday

6B • King Cat's corner

Topic
King Cat teaches the children to talk about what they do every day.

Aims
- To practice the present simple for routines.
- To teach the names of the days of the week.

Language
Present simple (routines)
I go home by bus/car/bike/on foot.
I go to school.
do my homework, play soccer, watch TV
Days of the week
What's next?
go swimming, go to my music lesson, go to my friend's house, sleep

What you need
- CD and player.

Before you begin
Tell the children about your day, miming actions to convey or reinforce meaning. Use some of the phrases in the book, and add more if you wish.

STUDENT'S BOOK

> *Classroom language and answer key*

 Tell your friend about your day.   12 minutes

Read through the phrases with the children and ask some children to talk about their day. They will almost certainly have other things they would like to say. It is important to keep this simple, but as far as possible, help them to say what they want to say. Some other phrases for "after school" activities are:

*I go to the park. I go to my Grandma's house. I go to my basketball lesson.
I play with my friends. I go to my mother's/father's office.*

The children then work in pairs to tell each other.

> *Tell us about your day.*

 Chant with me!   12 minutes

First, talk about different days of the week. Ask the children some questions: *What day is it today? When do we have our English class? What days are you here at school? What's your favorite day? Why?* and teach them the names of the days as they give answers.

Read through the words of the chant with the children. Then play the recording and get them to chant with it. The chant is circular – when you get to Sunday, it can start again.

Further practice: Activity Book Exercise 1.

> *Let's learn the names of the days.
> Repeat after me.*

6B • King Cat's corner

Let's read.
Look. This is King Cat going to school / swimming / his music lesson (etc.).

Close your books.
Listen. Check the correct day.

> **Answers**
> *Mondays:* go to school, go swimming
> *Tuesdays:* go to school, go to my friend's house
> *Wednesdays:* go to school, go to my music lesson
> *Thursdays:* go to school, go swimming
> *Fridays:* go to school, go to my friend's house
> *Saturdays:* sleep
> *Sundays:* sleep

Tell us about your week.

> **Answer**
> *Question:* What is your favorite day at school?

> **Answers**
> *swimming:* Mondays.
> *soccer:* Tuesdays.
> *music lesson:* Wednesdays.
> *TV:* Thursdays. *farm:* Saturdays.
> *homework:* Sundays.

> **Answers**
> 2 After school, I do my homework. 3 I go home by bus. 4 I go to school by bike.

3  Listen to what I do. Check the correct day.   10 minutes

Before you play the recording, read through the actions in the chart with the children. Check that they can remember them by holding up Vocabulary Cards 92–96. At first, say part of each phrase yourself (e.g. *Go to ...?*) and elicit the rest. Then hold up the cards again and get the children to say the phrases themselves.

Ask them to close their books the first time they listen and then ask what things they remember.

Play the recording again, and let the children check their answers. They could do this in pairs. In this case, pause the recording after every few sentences and give them time to talk together about their answers.

> **Tapescript**
> Hello! This is King Cat! Let me tell you about my week. On Mondays I go swimming. I like swimming! On Tuesdays, I go to my friend's house. We play soccer. On Wednesdays, I go to my music lesson. I play the trumpet. Listen! On Thursdays, I go swimming again and on Fridays, I go to my friend's house again. I go to school on Mondays, Tuesdays, Wednesdays, Thursdays, and Fridays! On Saturdays and Sundays I sleep!

Further practice: Activity Book Exercise 2.

4 Tell the class about your week.   10 minutes

The children can now tell the class about what they do each day. Choose a different child for each day. They can say: *On Mondays, I go ...* and use the words in King Cat's chart. If there is time, you could get them to write about one or two days in their notebooks.

Further practice: Activity Book Exercises 3 and 4.

ACTIVITY BOOK

1 Draw lines to show the correct order.   10 minutes

The children have to draw a line that follows the order of the days, starting from Monday. This makes a question, and they write their answer.

2 Read about Steve's week. Write the days.   15 minutes

New language: the next day, It's great fun!

Read through Steve's words with the children. You may need to give them some help to understand *the next day*. They read the text again and write the day under each picture.

3 Draw lines.   10 minutes

Again, read through the sentences with the children and check that they understand.

4 Write about your day.

Before the children write, ask them what they can say about their day. They can look back to the sentences in Exercises 2 and 3 for help, and you can write some examples on the board: *I go home by bus. After school, I play soccer.*

3  Listen to what I do. Check the correct day.

On Mondays, I ...

	go to school	go swimming	go to my music lesson	go to my friend's house	sleep!
Monday					
Tuesday					
Wednesday					
Thursday					
Friday					
Saturday					
Sunday					

 4 Tell the class about your week.

On Mondays, I go swimming.

6C Come back, Kip!

1  Listen and follow.

1 What is it, Mickey?

2 There's a cave here. Come and see! There's something in there.

3 Wow! I like the car!
Fantastic!
Kip! Come back!

4 Kip, stop! Help me!
Vrrooom!

5 I can't stop the car. Wait a minute! What's this?
Kip! Stop! Come back!

6 Hhhheeeeeelp!
Welcome back, Kip!
Goodbye, car!

Where's the car now? Find out in American English Primary Colors Book 3!

6C • Come back, Kip!

Topic
Tom, Mickey, and Kip are on the cliff edge. Mickey takes Tom to see a cave where he discovers a fantastic car. This is what the map was for! He calls the children to see it. Kip jumps into the car but it takes off into the air. Kip is thrown out, and the children watch the car disappear into the distance. (Where did it go? Find out in *American English Primary Colors* 3!)

Aims
- General language review.

Language
Review
There's a …
I like …
I can't …
What's this?

New language
Come and see.
Wait a minute!
Welcome back.
What can Kip see?
What can they do?
cave, something, fantastic, new

What you need
- CD and player.

Before you begin
This is the last episode, so you might want to go back over the story.

- *Using the mother tongue:* You can ask how Nick and Jess met each person. (Joanne: they crashed into a house. Zara: they were out in the snow. Nick thought her dogs were bears. Tom: birds attacked the balloon and it crashed into a tree. Ben: a giant wave pulled the balloon into the sea and he rescued them from the sharks.)

- *Without using the mother tongue:* You can ask some questions:

  Nick and Jess see many places in the story. What places? (*A town, a farm, mountains, an island.*)
  Kip finds something in the beginning. What is it? (*The map.*)
  Where does Joanne live? (*In a town.*)
  Where does Zara live? (*In the mountains.*)
  Where does Tom live? (*On a farm.*)
  Where does Ben live? (*On an island, in a tree house.*)
  Where does Mickey live? (*With Ben.*)
  Who is your favorite?

STUDENT'S BOOK

 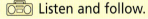   15 minutes

LISTENING TO THE STORY The children will probably have already looked at the end of the story, so you can let them have their books open while you play the recording. Then read through the pictures with them. Instead of comprehension questions, you can ask them about what they think: *Do you like caves? Look at the car! Do you like it? Is Kip very smart? Is he a good dog? Kip is safe! That's good.*

ACTING OUT Divide the class into pairs or small groups and get them to read the dialog.

Then ask some children to act out the story (eight parts: Jess, Nick, Joanne, Zara, Tom, Ben, Mickey, and Kip). They can read from their books or you could write the dialog or some prompts on the board. If possible, arrange chairs to make a "car" that Kip can jump into.

Classroom language and answer key

Listen to the story. Follow the pictures in your book.

Work in pairs.
Read the words.

I need a lot of children!
I need 8 children.
Who wants to be Jess? (etc.)

6C • Come back, Kip!

Example answers

1 He can see an island, trees, the sea, coconuts, a mountain, the children, the sky, sharks ...
2 In the sea. On an island. In the sky. In a town.
3 They can yell *Help!* They can write a message [new word]. They can make a boat. They can swim (but there are sharks!).

Let's sing a song.
Let's read the words first.

2 Think and tell the class.   5 minutes

Here the children use their imagination and give their own ideas. This is a free exercise for discussion, and you will need to help with new language to allow the children to express their ideas.

- *Picture 1:* Encourage the children to imagine. Kip is up in the sky – very, very high. What can he see?
- *Picture 2:* The car is flying away in the picture – where could it be now?
- The children do not have a balloon. They do not have a car. They do not have a boat. What can they do?

If your class is continuing on to the next level in the course, you can tell them that they will find out what happens to the car then.

Further practice: Activity Book Exercise 1.

3 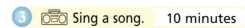 Sing a song.   10 minutes

This final song is similar to the song in *Welcome!* C. Read through the words with the children. Play the recording and encourage the children to sing with it.

EXTRA IDEA   To end the story, you could play "Treasure hunt" (see *Extra activities*, pages T81–T82 in the Teacher's Book). You can make some clues and have a prize at the end – preferably, a small prize for everyone.

Further practice: Activity Book Exercises 2 and 3.

ACTIVITY BOOK

1 What can Kip see? Write the words.   10 minutes

Look at the picture with the children and get them to tell you what they can see. They then use the list of words to label the things and animals in the picture.

2 Think. What can they do? Are they good ideas or bad ideas? Check the boxes.   10 minutes

There are no "correct" answers to this exercise – but you can ask the children for their reasons. Here are some possible ideas and reasons:

- *They can yell:* Bad idea – nobody can hear them.
- *They can write a letter:* Bad idea – how can they send it? Good idea if they can find a bottle.
- *They can swim:* Bad idea – there are sharks!
- *They can make a boat:* Good idea – they can make a boat with coconut trees.
- *They can fly:* Bad idea – they can't fly!
- *They can jump:* Bad idea – they can't jump far.

3 Think. Where's the car now? Draw a picture and write about your idea.   15 minutes

The children can use their own imagination and draw what they want. Help them to write a few words about *their* ideas. For example: *I think the car is in the sea. I think the car is in a tree.*

Think and tell the class.

What can Kip see?   Where's the car now?   What can they do now?

 Sing a song.

Up, up, up,
Up in a balloon.
Up, up, up,
Up in a balloon.

Let's go!
Let's go!

Let's go to see new friends.
Let's go to see new places.
Let's go to see new things.

Goodbye!

6D • Storytime: The cages

Topic
A man and a woman are catching birds to sell. Their boat is in a storm and they become lost. A parrot arrives and says he can help them find the way home – but he won't do it. He says, "You want to go home – my friends want to go home too." The man and woman understand that all creatures want to be free. They release the birds and the parrot guides them home.

Aims
- To develop the children's listening and speaking fluency.
- To review language covered in the course.

Language
Review
Numbers
can, can't
I can't find …
I don't know
I can help you.
You have …

New language
You want to …
We / My friends want to …
He's right
cage, excellent, terrible, free, parrot, paper clip

What you need
- CD and player.
- Copies of Cut-out 9 (Teacher's Book, page T125) for Exercise 2.
- Scissors, posterboard, markers, glue, and paper clips for Exercise 2.
- Optional: a ready-made parrot for Exercise 2.

Before you begin
As before, you could change the order of the exercises and get the children to make their parrots before they listen to the story.

STUDENT'S BOOK

  Listen and follow. 10 minutes

Classroom language and answer key

You can start by telling the story while the children look at the pictures. Point to the pictures and slowly say what is happening. For example:

1 Look. There are two people. A man and a woman. They have a boat. And they have a lot of birds. Look! The birds are in cages.
2 Now they're in the sea. The sea is terrible. Look! They don't know where to go. They can't find the map!
3 The sea is quiet. But they are lost. The man says, "Where are we?" The woman says, "I don't know."
4 "This is terrible!" they say. They yell, "Help! Help!"
5 Look! A bird comes. It's a parrot. The parrot says, "I can tell you the way." "Good!" says the man. "Tell us!" "No!" says the parrot.
6 The parrot says, "You have my friends."
7 They don't understand. "What?" they say. The parrot says, "You want to go home. My friends want to go home, too."
8 "He's right," says the woman. The birds want to be free. Everybody wants to be free. They open the cages. The birds can fly home.
9 The parrot tells them the way. They say, "Thank you. And no cages!" No more cages.

Let me tell you a story.
Look at the pictures.
Look at picture 1.

Play the recording once or twice while the children follow the story in their books. Then divide the class into threes (the man, the woman, and the parrot) to read the dialog.

Listen. Follow the story in your books.
Work together. Read the story.

6D • The cages

Cut out the picture of the parrot. Be careful!
Glue the parrot on the posterboard.
Color the parrot.
Cut around the parrot.
Put some paper clips here.
Add some more paper clips.

Who wants to act out the story?

Answers
Tuesday, Wednesday, Friday, Saturday, Sunday

Answers
Seven children go to school by bus. Four children go to school by bike. Nine children go to school by car. Six children go to school on foot.
Ten children go home by bus. Four children go home by bike. Seven children go home by car. Five children go home on foot.

---

2 Make a parrot.   20+ minutes

Use Cut-out 9, page T125 in the Teacher's Book.

This activity requires careful control of scissors. The more the children do, the better, but make sure they use children's scissors. Some questions to consider:
- Should the children glue the cut-out to the posterboard or should you?
- Should the children cut out the parrot themselves, or should you?

They will need to experiment with the paper clips to make the parrot balance.

3 Act out the story. Use your parrot.   10 minutes

You can now ask some children to act out the story (three parts). The group can balance one of their parrots on the back of a chair, and a child can speak for it. You can put prompts or the whole dialog on the board.

ACTIVITY BOOK Review

1 Write the days.   5 minutes

The children write the names of the missing days on the bridges.

2 Talk about the charts.   10 minutes

Note: This exercise needs to be done in class.

The children may be familiar with this kind of chart from other school work.

3 Make a chart about your class.   10+ minutes

Note: This exercise needs to be done in class.

You can ask *Who comes to school by bus?* etc., and build up a chart on the board. If you have a small class, they could ask children in other classes.

4 Write about your chart.   15+ minutes

Ask the children what they can say about the chart. Ask them to write a few sentences following the model of the ones they wrote in Exercise 2.

I can …   5 minutes

Before the children color in the stars, go through some examples. Get them to say what they like to eat, the days of the week, and what they do every day.

Picture Dictionary 6   10 minutes

The children can now complete Picture Dictionary 6 on page 63.

EXTRA PRACTICE Optional work is on pages T100 and T101 in the Teacher's Book.

Answers
1 ice cream, milk, apples, fish
2 a pencil case, a bag, a cake, a coconut, bananas, colored pencils, a ruler, a notebook
3 Wednesdays, Thursdays, Fridays, Saturdays, Sundays
4 a Thursday b Wednesday c Tuesday d Friday e Monday f Saturday, Sunday
5 On Tuesdays, I go to my friend's house. On Thursdays, I sing. On Fridays, I watch TV. On Saturdays, I play in the park. On Sundays, I sleep.

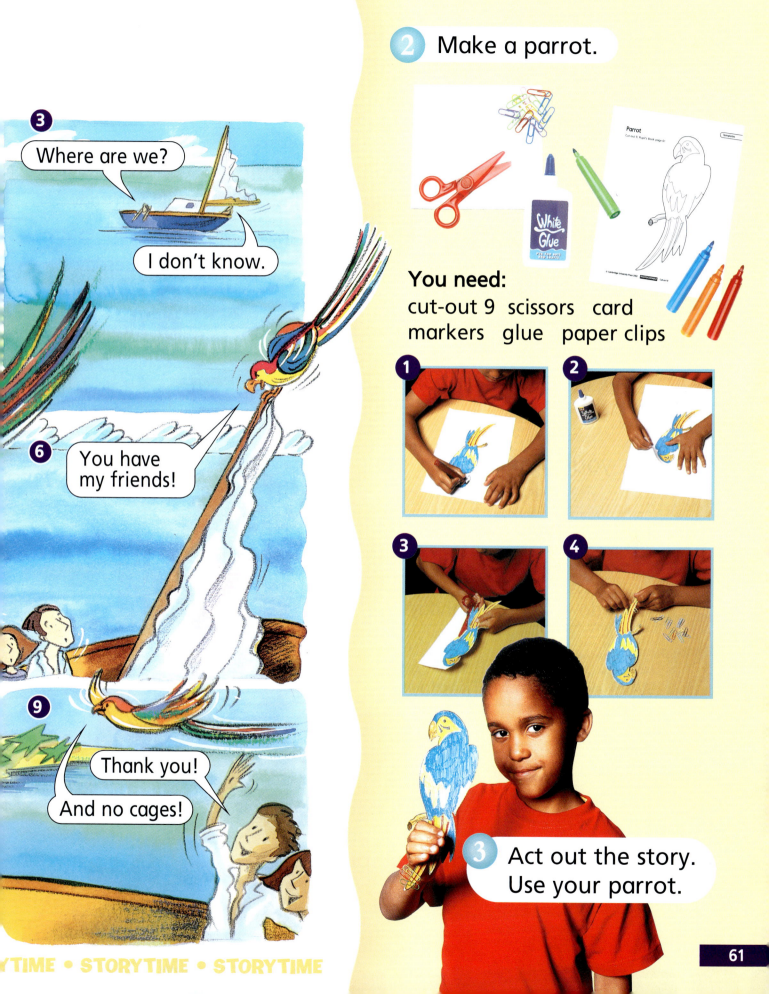

Review

1 What are their favorite days?

1. King Cat's favorite day is the day after Tuesday.
2. Jess's favorite day is the day before Thursday.
3. Ben's favorite day is the day before Tuesday.
4. Nick's favorite day is the day after Friday.
5. Kip's favorite day is the day after Monday.
6. Joanne's favorite day is the day before Saturday.

a. Wednesday
b. Saturday
c. Wednesday
d. Tuesday
e. Friday
f. Monday

What's your favorite day?

2 Ask your friend.

What do you do after school?

What do you do on Mondays?

What do you do on Tuesdays?

What do you do on ... ?

3 Play the game with your spinner.

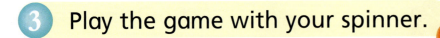

Review

Topic
This section contains review exercises and a board game.

Aim
- To review the language covered in Units 5 and 6.

Language
Review
Days of the week.
Present simple for routines:
On Monday, I …
Do you like …?

New language
the day after
the day before

What you need
- CD and player.
- The children need their spinners for Activity Book Exercise 3.

STUDENT'S BOOK

1 What are their favorite days? 10 minutes

Read through the sentences with the children and check that they understand *the day after* and *the day before*. Let them work in pairs to work out the days. They write the sentence number (1–6) beside each day. When they have finished, ask for the answers.

2 Ask your friend. 5 minutes

Ask some children the questions in the book and help them to answer in complete sentences. Then put the class in pairs to practice. You can get some pairs to ask and answer in front of the class.

Classroom language and answer key

Answers
1 a or c   2 c or a   3 f
4 b   5 d   6 e

Review

3 **Play the game with your spinner.** 20+ minutes

Note: This exercise has to be done in class. The children need their spinners.

The children will need their spinners from Activity Book *Welcome!* C to play this game. They will need a game piece or a coin to show where they are on the board.

The game works in the same way as the game in Unit 2 *Review*.
Divide the class into pairs or threes and explain how to play.

1. Everyone puts their game pieces on *Start*.
2. The players take turns spinning their spinners and moving the game pieces forward according to the number they get when it lands. They should say this number, and count their moves forward aloud.
3. When they land on a tile, they have to follow an instruction or answer a question. If they can't do it, the others in the group can help (there is no penalty for not knowing the answer).
4. The tiles with arrows mean "Go forward" or "Go back" the number of tiles shown on the arrow.
5. To finish, a player must land on *Finish* with the exact number. If the spinner shows a number that is too big to finish, the player counts into *Finish* and back out again.

Make a balloon mobile.

Page 64 of the Activity Book has an additional craft idea which the children might like to make at home. This is a balloon mobile.

- Hand out photocopies of Cut-out 10 on page T126 in the Teacher's Book.
- Look at page 64 with the children and go through the instructions. Explain that they can make the mobile at home, with their family or friends.
- You could invite them to bring their mobiles into class when they are ready, and make a display.
- If you use the same classroom all the time, you could hang the finished mobiles up in the classroom.
- You could make this mobile in class if you prefer.

Instructions

1. Color the eight balloons in four different colors (two balloons for each color).
2. Glue the balloons onto posterboard.
3. Cut them out.
4. Tape pieces of string on the back of four different-colored balloons.
5. Glue the matching balloons back to back, with the string between them.
6. Tape two pencils together in a cross shape.
7. Attach the strings from the balloons to the ends of the pencils.
8. Hang up your balloon mobile.

Word lists

Welcome!
a
bag
balloon
bus
car
cat
classroom
dog
go
Goodbye.
Hello.
house
Is it a ...?
It's a ...
Let's ...!
marker
my
My ...'s in my ...
My name's ...
notebook
Oh, no.
park
pen
pencil
pencil case
ruler
school
street
sky
town
up
What is it?
What's that?
What's your name?
Where's ...?
Yes.
your

1 Hello, Kip!
banana
book
but
cake
Come on!
cupcake
door
drink
eraser
farm
favorite
floor
good
Here you are.
I don't know.
It's a ...
Lift off!
lunchbox
map

nice
Numbers: 1–10
open
planet
Point to the ...
run
sandwich
scissors
see
spaceship
Stand up tall.
stop
straw
sweet
tape
Thanks.
they're
tummy
wall
What's in your ...?
What's this?
Where's my ...?
yummy

2 Hello, Joanne!
ask
big
birthday party
children
clap
classroom
desk
friend
Good morning.
hat
he
Help!
he's
her
here
he's/she's (eight)
Hi!
his
hop
How old are you?
How old is he/she?
I like ...
I'm (seven).
It's (big).
jump
Look!
magic
me
mouse
No, it isn't.
now
Numbers: 11–15
paper
party

place
our
she
(six) and (seven)
are ...
teacher
That's my ...
there
This is my ...
Welcome.
We're here.
What's her/his name?
Where are you/we?
Where's ...?
with
Yes, it is.
you

3 Hello, Zara!
Are you/they ...?
ball
bear
black
blue
boy
brown
Can you (help me)?
cold
color
Come down.
dangerous
down
elephant
garden
girl
glue
green
hot
house
I know.
I'm not.
in
Is (Daniel) in a (balloon)?
kick
man
No, he isn't.
No, they aren't.
Of course.
on
red
round
skis
small
snow
strong
There is ...
There are ...

They aren't ...
tree
trumpet
up
very
white
yell
yellow
Yes, he is.
Yes, I am.
Yes, they are.

4 Hello, Tom!
bird
can
can't
chick
climb (up)
count to
cow
Dad
dinner time
drive
duck
everything
fast
fly
Get out!
Go away!
go out
hear
hen
high
horse
I can see ...
legs
listen
mask
Mom
Numbers: 15–20
OK
rain
read
silly
sing
smart
stay
string
swim
telephone
Thank you.
umbrella
walk
What can we do?
write

5 Hello, Ben!
animal
blond

boat
brother
catch
close
Come here!
crocodile
Don't worry.
ear
eat
every day
eye
farm
fish
forest
fruit
grass
hair
have
head
He has ...
island
I have ...
live
long
monkey
mouth
nose
open
pat
posterboard
pull
river
safe
say
sea
shark
shark snapper
She has ...
ship
short
telescope
That's right!
That's wrong!
think
tiger
too
tree house
We have ...
Who are you?

6 Goodbye!
apple
Are you OK?
by bike
by bus
by car
cage
cave
cheese

coconut
Come and see.
Come back!
day
do my homework
Do you like ...?
Excellent!
Fantastic!
Follow me.
free
Friday
go
go home
go swimming
go to my friend's house
go to my music lesson
go to school
Here we are.
He's right.
home
I can't find ...
ice cream
I like ...
I'm OK.
Let me think.
milk
Monday
music lesson
new
No, I don't.
on foot
orange
paper clip
parrot
pear
play soccer
Saturday
sleep
something
Sunday
Tell us.
terrible
thing
Thursday
Tuesday
Wait a minute!
want to
watch TV
Wednesday
week
Welcome back!
What's next?
Why is it ...?
Wow.
Yes, I do.

A–Z: teaching young learners

Note that words like this: **motivation** indicate a cross-reference.

Acting out

What and why?
Most children enjoy the physical activity involved in drama and role play, and there are opportunities throughout the course for acting out stories. Acting out requires practice in pairs or groups and should allow the children some freedom of interpretation so that they can include other language or other ideas if they want to. Acting out should be a creative task rather than merely a reproductive one. It provides a way of making learning more memorable.

Practical ideas
- After the children have heard the stories from you and on the CD, write the key phrases on the board and practice them with the class as a whole so that they understand what they mean and how to say them.
- Acting out in groups means working together. It is not always easy for young children to work together, so it may be best to add a preparation stage to ease the process. Start by allocating each child in the class a character – so, for example, if there are four characters acting out, divide the class into four groups, each group having the same role. In pairs or threes, the children prepare their role together so they are working on the same task and providing ideas and support for each other. Ask the children to write their character's name or draw a picture, to show which role they are taking. Then, when they are ready, move the children so that they are with the other three characters. They can then prepare their drama together.
- Some children will want to act out their drama in front of the class with the use of props – dress-up clothes, masks, or hats – and others will prefer to stay in their seats and speak the dialogs. However, encourage the children to experiment and work with different companions.
- Acting out is really only beneficial to those doing the acting. Children generally like doing it, but the time they are waiting can be time wasted. It is best, therefore, to limit the amount of time for each performance.
- If you ask some groups to act out in front of the class, make sure that others have their turn next time – if they want to. You could put the names of groups into a hat and draw one out at random, or you could rotate around the classroom so that groups know when it is their turn.
- Some children feel very shy about acting out in front of the class. Sometimes they just need encouragement, as they really would like to do it. Sometimes, however, they really don't want to do it. In these cases, you have to be very sensitive to the feelings of the children and not push them too much.

Craft activities

What and why?
In the *Storytime* section of each unit, and in some exercises in the Activity Book, children have the opportunity to make objects related to the story. These are designed to help them become more involved in the stories, to encourage their hand-eye co-ordination, and to help them learn language in a meaningful context. Craft activities also enable children to take the language out of the classroom and build a bridge with the world outside. Children learn how to cut, trace, copy, fold, and color as well as how to follow instructions. Craft activities also have a very important role in making learning more memorable, by associating it with a tangible object. You may feel that you don't have time for craft activities. However, many teachers have found that they make a lot of difference to the participation of the children and their positive view of the classroom – all of which can have a significant impact on **motivation**.

A–Z: teaching young learners

Practical ideas

- Before the lesson, take time to follow the instructions in the Student's Book, Activity Book, or in the Teacher's Book, and make the craft item yourself. This way you can establish where any problems may arise, how long to allow for the activity, and what equipment and space you need.
- Show the finished craft item to the children before they start.
- Before starting the activity, make sure that the children have enough space on their desks or tables. Ask them to clear the desk of all other books, etc. It is often useful to spread newspapers on the desks for craft activities – this will not only protect against glue or paint spillage but will also establish that this is a different kind of English activity.
- Make sure that any tools the children use are not dangerous. Scissors, for example, should be children's scissors.
- Allow time for the children to look at the pictures of the activity in the book. It may be useful to have a poster on the wall with pictures to show the meanings of key words such as *cut* (scissors), *trace* (tracing paper), *fold* (a piece of paper being folded), *color* (markers), etc.
- Encourage children to work in pairs or small groups. You can experiment with different compositions of the groups – for example, boys and girls working together, or boys and girls in separate groups. While the children are working, go round and help, but work on your own model at the same time so that the children can see what needs to be done. Sit with the children at their desk and do the actions with them.
- If the children are making craft items that they will need for future lessons (such as the hats or masks, for example), make sure they write their names on them. Keep them in a special box or cupboard in the classroom so they can be found easily.
- Allow time at the end of the lesson for the children to put things away. This provides a useful opportunity for additional language experience. For example: *Put the glue in here, please. Put the newspaper in the garbage. Put the hats over here to dry. Write your names on the back. Who can help me put the paper away?*

You can find more craft ideas in the *Extra activities* section in the Teacher's Book.

Discipline

What and why?

Many teachers find that the most difficult part of their job is maintaining discipline. "If they'd just behave, I might be able to teach them something!" is a common complaint. The first thing to consider is: do you really have a discipline problem? Many "discipline problems" are not problems at all – it is often the teacher's reaction that makes it a problem. We cannot expect 100% attention all the time, particularly from young children – in fact we would have very good reason to be worried if children always did everything we asked them to do! When teaching young children, it is important to be flexible and patient, and to allow "children to be children."

In some cases, however, real discipline problems arise. There can be many reasons for this but there are three very common ones. Firstly, discipline problems are often the result of boredom. Bored children lose **motivation**, and unmotivated children often misbehave. Secondly, discipline problems often derive from feelings of failure, and a lack of involvement, and are a way of protecting the child's own self-image. Thirdly, discipline problems are fundamentally about the *relationship* between the teacher and the children. If the children feel that the teacher doesn't know what he/she is doing, or is not in charge, they will often take advantage of the comparative freedom that this gives them.

Practical ideas

- Boredom is probably a lot more common than we realize. Feelings of boredom often come from a lack of personal control in the classroom when children feel they are always being told what to do. Children who take part in making real decisions about what happens in the classroom are more involved and have greater motivation. They are less bored and less likely to create discipline problems.

A–Z: teaching young learners

- If you see a child who is starting to "sink" – a child who is losing motivation through feelings of failure, try to give that child some extra personal attention. Ask them how they are doing, if they found something difficult, and so on to show that you value them.
- Often, a particularly disruptive child is really asking for help and attention. As far as possible, it is best to avoid getting into a negative cycle of misbehavior – punishment – escalating misbehavior. Personal contact with the child, listening, talking, finding out what is wrong, and how you can help, will likely be more productive.
- Discipline problems can also arise from feelings of low self-esteem. In the long term, you need to try to build up the child's feelings of success by giving them things that you know they can do. In the short term, you can raise self-esteem by giving a disruptive child special responsibilities, such as collecting work, checking that everyone has everything they need, returning equipment to its place, and so on.
- When discipline problems continually occur in class, it is usually fruitful to involve the children in suggesting how things can be improved. For example, it is probably better to say *Our group work isn't working. What can we do about it?* than to say *Stop messing around! The next person who does that …*
- The key to a balanced, happy working environment is a positive relationship between the children and the teacher, and the feeling that both parties are working in the same direction. Many teachers involve the children in drawing up a "code of conduct" for their classroom, or "rules for our group work," that the children can suggest themselves. When things break down, this then puts the teacher in a less confrontational role with the children.
- Young children, however, do need to feel that the teacher is "in charge." Few, if any, children are "bad." Children are in the process of finding themselves, of shaping their relations with others, and of experimenting with their behavior. They need, therefore, to discover the limits of acceptable behavior. A good teacher is one who is firm but not inflexible, who expects the children to be well-behaved and who signals that serious misbehavior won't be tolerated, and explains why.
- Discipline problems can also occur because of the energy levels of the children. Sitting at a desk for long periods of time often produces restlessness. You may find it useful to start a lesson with some physical activity (such as a "Simon says" game – see page T81 in the Teacher's Book) to release the energy that the children have. Alternatively, they may be feeling tired and unable to concentrate, in which case it will probably be impossible to get them to do any real "work." The important thing is to judge each situation individually and to take a flexible approach.
- Punishing children should be considered a last resort. Punishment rarely makes things better, and often makes them a lot worse. More can usually be achieved by explaining why certain actions are not acceptable and by building an agreement with the child about how the situation can be improved. If a child becomes so disruptive that he/she is disturbing others, then it is probably better to withdraw that child for the sake of the class, but the general direction to take must be to encourage the child to regulate his or her own behavior.

English and the mother tongue

What and why?

Knowing when to use the mother tongue and when to use English in a classroom is one of the hardest decisions to make. In the past, many writers have recommended that teachers should *only* use English – that the mother tongue, in other words, should not be allowed. This is not a view we take, especially for young learners. Firstly, it is impossible to learn anything unless you relate it to what you already know. This means that children will *always* translate even if we tell them not to. It is important, then, that we make sure they have the *correct* translation. The old argument about "encouraging them to think in English" is only really feasible when they have enough language with which to think. For elementary school children, this is unlikely to be the case with a foreign language for a very long

A–Z: teaching young learners

time. Secondly, it is important that the children have a sense of security in the classroom, that they feel they can ask for help, explain problems, say how they feel, and so on. They will only do this in the mother tongue. Thirdly, using the mother tongue means that it is possible to do more interesting work and more complex types of activities.

There is, of course, a danger in this – that the children will hear very little English. Every situation is unique, but a general principle might be to try to use English as much as possible – without producing confused, worried, or bored learners.

Practical ideas

- Give instructions in English, but repeat them in the mother tongue. After a while, you could give an English instruction and get the children to say it in the mother tongue, so that you know they have understood.
- Give instructions in English, but try to use as much gesture as possible to make the meaning clear. In the craft activities, for example, the children can *hear* an instruction in English and *see* what it means.
- Give instructions in English, but allow time for the children to "process" the language before you give another instruction. Comprehension is improved by giving the children *time* between statements, not by speaking more slowly.
- Only use the mother tongue at certain times. For example, when you are **previewing** or when you are helping the children to understand something new.
- Try to use the same language again and again. The "Classroom language" section in the teaching notes for each unit gives examples.
- Teach the children the meaning of classroom language that you will use a lot. For example: *Work in pairs. Open your book. Listen and follow.* You could put a poster on the wall with common phrases that you use, and their meanings. When you give an instruction, you can point to the poster at the same time.
- Teach the children some phrases that they can use. For example: *I don't understand. Please say it again. I can't hear. What's the English for ...?*

Games

What and why?

Games are a very important part of a successful route to language learning for young learners. They are useful in a number of ways: in maintaining **motivation**, in giving a natural context for using English, and in providing variety within a lesson.

Practical ideas

- While the children will enjoy the "game" aspect of the activity, it is important that they understand that it is not just for fun. Before you start a game, explain how it will help them to learn. For example, *We can play a game now. This will help you remember the new words.*
- The *Extra activities* section in this Teacher's Book includes some games that you can play with the class, and some notes on using games. A reference to a suitable game is given in the teaching notes for many units.
- It is important to make sure that all the children understand how to play the game. Explain in **English and the mother tongue**, and then get the children to tell *you* how to play. Also, demonstrate with some children in front of the class.
- After you have played a game successfully, you can ask the children to suggest variations on the game, or to suggest new games. You could have a "suggestion box" in class for this.
- Include a game in different parts of the lesson – not always at the end. A game shouldn't be seen as a "reward" for hard work, but another way of learning.
- After the children have played a game, ask them if they liked it, how they could play it better, or how they would improve upon it.
- Board games are a useful way of reviewing language. You can ask the children to make their own – for example, they could make a board game similar to the ones in the *Review* sections in the Student's Book.

A–Z: teaching young learners

- Games can get out of hand! It is important to make sure that the children don't get too excited, or you may find that you have **discipline** problems destroying something intended to be enjoyable. When they are playing a game, go around the class and maintain a lively but purposeful atmosphere. If some children become extremely noisy, stop the game and calm them down.

Homework

What and why?

Homework serves many useful purposes in learning, although few children would agree! It helps to keep the children in contact with what they are learning, especially when their lessons are only once or twice a week. It also provides an opportunity for the individual child to focus on his or her personal work, outside the classroom. Language learning is a slow process, so some work outside the classroom is always useful.

Practical ideas

- It is important to remember that a young child's life is often very full. They usually return home from school very tired, and the last thing they want to do is more school work. Small amounts of homework, taking approximately 20 miniutes at a time, are best. More than that can have a negative effect on the child's attitude towards learning English.
- The Activity Book provides many exercises that the children can do alone. Before you ask them to do an exercise at home, however, it is important that you go through it with them in class. This helps the children to *remember* to do the exercise and understand what they have to do in order to complete it.
- If you give homework, it is important that you spend some time going over it in class. This is to make sure that the children realize that you think it is important.
- If you can, it is a good idea to discuss the idea of homework with the children in their mother tongue. Explain to them how it can help them – they need to understand that it is for their benefit, not yours! You could also come to an agreement with the children about how much homework they should have, and what day would be the best for them.
- If it is possible, you can encourage the children to do their homework with a friend. It may be more motivating if they see it as a *social* experience.
- Try to give a choice of homework exercises. The more the children can *choose*, the more involved they will be. You can also ask them to suggest homework exercises.

Large classes

What and why?

Large classes of 25+ children require careful classroom management strategies. Make sure that the children are involved in the tasks and can hear the recording – they should be able to see the board and you! Large classes often create two kinds of problems – the first is **discipline** and the second is non-involvement which leads to lack of **motivation**. Discipline problems may arise in large classes because children may recognize that English lessons are different in style and approach from other lessons and may feel that their behavior can be less disciplined, without the teacher seeing what they are doing. It is important to establish that although there are "fun" activities in English lessons, they are important for learning and can be more fun if everyone can hear the teacher and understand what is happening. Motivation problems often come about because some children feel lost and alone in a large class, without any personal contact with the teacher. This is especially true if the children are slightly deaf, have poor eyesight, or have **special needs**.

Both of these aspects mean that it is important to find ways of "breaking down" the size of a large class and to make personal contact more possible.

A–Z: teaching young learners

Practical ideas

- In large classes, the more capable children often sit at the front of the class, while weaker ones sit at the back to try to "hide" from the teacher. This can cause weaker students to get weaker, as they see themselves as "less able" and lose **motivation**. It is important, then, to move the children around, so that the ones at the back sometimes sit at the front. For example, you could rotate everyone around each week.
- If you have a very large class with the children sitting in rows, you can give each row *across* a name and each row *down* a different name. When you ask a question, you can say the name of a row, and a child in that row can answer.
- Despite the fact that there are many people in the classroom, learning in a large class can mean learning alone. It is very easy for the quieter child not to be noticed. It is important, then, to divide a large class into groups so that they can identify and interact with a smaller number of people. You can ask each group to give themselves a name, so that you can refer to them as a group. Groups can have the same members over a period of time – perhaps a few weeks. If you change the composition of groups, you can ask them to give themselves a new name. You could vary the kind of name that the groups have – for example, they could have names of animals or sports or colors, etc.
- You could make a timetable of when you will talk personally to each group, perhaps when the other children are getting on with some other work. One key factor in the success of the children is the fact that someone cares that they are learning. Personal contact and interest in their work are extremely important.
- Groups can each choose a representative. The other children can then tell their representative if they have suggestions, want extra practice, etc.
- Songs, craft activities, and drama all generate noise. If you need to talk to a child when the class is working rather noisily, it is best to say the child's name quietly (children can hear their name in a noisy classroom) or approach the child and speak quietly. Shouting will raise the noise and stress levels. Children's noise will always rise above a teacher's shouting.
- If you would like to have the attention of the whole class, it is worth having a word combined with an action which you can say quietly (perhaps say *Balloon!* and put your hand up in the air). When children hear this word and see this action, they will know they should stop what they are doing and listen to you.

Mixed abilities

What and why?

Children bring different experiences and expectations with them to school. They will have different expectations about learning and classroom behavior. It is likely, then, that even from the start, there will be differences in approach, attitude, aptitude, and ability in the English language classroom. The larger the class, the greater these differences may appear, and because of these differences we cannot expect that all the children will be interested in or able to do the same tasks in the same way at the same time. It is important not to confuse the two aspects of "ability": ability *in English*, and ability *to learn*. A poor ability in English does not mean that, with the right support, the child does not have the ability to learn. Many teachers talk about a child's *aptitude to language learning*. In fact, aptitude to language learning is probably the least significant factor in classroom language learning. If a person has learned one language, they can learn another. The key here is a child's aptitude to *specific ways of being taught*. A child's poor rate of learning may therefore say more about what is happening in the classroom than it does about the child.

Practical ideas

- Apparent differences in ability are often not differences in ability at all. They may be connected to differences in **motivation**.
- Not all children will work or learn at the same pace. It is useful to have extra puzzles or exercises ready for those children who finish a

task before the others. These can be written by the children – when they have completed an exercise, particularly in the Activity Book, they can create another similar exercise for other children. They can write the answers on the back and place it in a Puzzle Box. Children can take a puzzle or exercise from the Puzzle Box to complete while they are waiting.

- Particularly in **large classes**, it is important to have regular personal contact with the children. This will help you find out if they are keeping up with the rest of the class. Giving extra personal help to children when they first experience difficulties can stop bigger problems from developing later.
- At the end of a unit, you can allow time for the children to sit in small groups and go through what they have learned. You could form groups to make sure that some of the less capable children are placed with the more capable.
- Some children prefer to learn by writing and drawing. Others prefer to learn by handling objects. Where possible, allow children opportunities to practice new language with objects – perhaps Lego blocks, models of animals, toy cars, etc.
- Encourage children to bring items or ideas from home which link in with the units. Perhaps these can be displayed on a special table or window sill in class. Children who may not feel confident expressing themselves may prefer to show something.
- The aim is to help all children feel confident about language learning so it is better to wait until the individual child is ready before pushing them to speak or **act out** a drama in English.

Motivation

What and why?

Initially, the motivation of young learners is generally very high. Over time, many children lose their motivation, and may appear bored, tired, and unwilling to learn. Many teachers respond by looking for "fun" things to do – more games, songs, etc. These often help, but the effect is usually temporary because the basic situation causing the reduction in motivation has not changed.

There are many reasons why the motivation of children changes so much. Many of these reasons may be beyond the control of the English teacher – for example, family life, health, other school work, friendship, and so on. However, there are two significant aspects of what happens inside the classroom that can have a direct impact on the motivation level of children. Firstly, motivation is directly related to self-esteem. Children who have low levels of self-esteem do not commit themselves to learning. None of us want to fail, which is why failing students often *pretend* that they are not interested – they do this to protect their self-image. It is very important, therefore, that we try to help the children develop a positive image of themselves as language learners and create feelings of success, not failure. Secondly, motivation is directly related to a sense of being in control. As humans, we are always more committed to something if we have had a role in making a decision about it. It is also important, therefore, that children are involved, as intelligent, creative beings, in making decisions about what they are doing.

Practical ideas

- Try to make sure that the children have a clear idea of how much they have learned and a feeling that they are making progress. For example, look back on things you have done with them, not to review them, but to show how much they now understand. Say things like *Look! One month ago you couldn't understand that. Now you can!*
- Choose "larger tasks" that give the children more "psychological space" to plan their own work, set their own pace, and make their own decisions about what they do. For example, craft activities, group work, pair work and time to write, design, and draw can all create a feeling of more personal control.
- Include tasks that involve a personal response, as well as value and appreciate that personal response by giving personal feedback:

A–Z: teaching young learners

displaying the children's work, telling them how you have told someone else about the lovely work they have done, etc. Making posters or art designs, writing simple poems, making models, etc. can create feelings of pride in their work.

- Provide choice. Instead of saying *Do this*, say *You can choose. You can do this, this, or that*. This may be a choice of materials to use in a craft, a choice of whether they do something in writing or orally, a choice of what they do for homework, a choice of where they sit in the classroom, and so on.

- Involve the children in classroom decision-making. Many of the decisions that teachers make can be shared with the children without any risks to the course as whole. You might be able to share decisions about when homework is given, how long they will spend on a particular task, what they will do during the next class, who will do what and when, whether they are going to act out something, whether they are going to sing a song again, how you can decorate the classroom, and so on.

- Find out what the children think. Find out if they think they need more practice, if they have suggestions of their own, if they find things easy or difficult, boring or interesting, if they would like to do something again, and so on. You could place a "suggestion box" in your class, or write a guided letter so that children can complete it with their ideas.

- Think about how you give feedback. Even very young children quickly develop an image of themselves in the classroom and can usually identify who is the "best" in the class, who is the "weakest," etc. They do this by monitoring and comparing the feedback that the teacher gives to each child. This, of course, affects their view of themselves – and how capable they think they are. Make sure you give positive, encouraging feedback.

- In general, it is best to avoid getting into giving "rewards." Most research in this area shows that this can have the effect of devaluing the work that leads to the reward by making the child focus on external rewards rather than their own feelings of success and satisfaction. Also, rewards are only motivating if you get them sometimes – for those who don't get them, or who have very little prospect of getting one, a rewards system is anything but motivating. In games, for example, it is probably best to avoid giving points for correct answers. At such an early stage in learning, being "punished" for not knowing something is not very encouraging. A points system can be used, however, when it is obvious that points are earned because of "luck" – such as spinning a spinner.

Music

What and why?

Music can have a very beneficial role in teaching young learners. It can help to establish a classroom "atmosphere," it can make learning more memorable and it can give a sense of security and comfort to the children. **Songs and chants**, in particular, are very useful in developing confidence in English and giving practice, but instrumental music can also have a great effect in the classroom.

Practical ideas

- If you play music when you are **starting a lesson**, you can help the children to ease into their English class and make the "psychological switch" from what they were doing immediately before.

- Different types of music can be used to affect the pace that the students are working at. If, for example, they are working on a **craft activity**, you could play some soft classical music which will encourage them to work with care. If you want them to work quickly, you can choose faster, more rhythmic music.

- You can choose a variety of music as a background – for example, classical music, pop music, South American pipe music, Indian music. You could just briefly tell the children the name of the music and where it comes from.

- You could select different types of music from English-speaking countries: classical music, folk music, pop music, old music, modern music, etc.

- You could ask the students to suggest music.

A–Z: teaching young learners

Pair work and group work

What and why?

The time that children spend in English lessons is usually quite short. If they are only allowed to talk to the teacher, most children will not have the opportunity to say very much – if anything. Working in pairs or small groups means that more children have more opportunity to talk more. More importantly, however, children *need* the space and opportunity to be who they are. Group work in small groups or pair work gives them the "psychological space" to do this. It can give them the space to exchange ideas and to be creative. It can provide a change of pace and variety. Whole class work for a long time, especially with a **large class**, demands a lot of attention and concentration in one "mode" – more than most children are able to give. It is important to provide opportunities for group work or pair work, but it is equally important that this is set up correctly. If it isn't, you will almost certainly end up with classroom management problems!

Practical ideas

- Before the children work in pairs or groups, make sure they know exactly what they have to do. You can give the instructions in both **English and the mother tongue**, and you can give an example by asking one or two children in front of the class.
- While they are working, you can go around the class, listening and helping.
- It is usually best to limit the time for pair work. Make sure that the children have enough time to do the task and that the focus is clear. If you allow too much time, they will lose the focus and not see the point of what they are doing. It is equally important not to allow too little time. This can cause frustration and confusion.
- Make sure that any work that you ask them to do in pairs has a concrete focus – that what *you* expect it is clear to them. For example, set tasks that have a practical outcome, such as making a list of words or reading a dialog, rather than something very general such as discussing an idea.
- Some children will certainly finish before others. In this case, have short extra exercises available. The *King Cat's fun pages* in the Activity Book can be used for this purpose.
- Small groups can give themselves a name, such as the name of a color or an animal. If groups re-form from time to time, they can choose a new name. See **Large classes**.

Physical action

What and why?

Physical movement is very important for young learners in a number of ways. Firstly, children probably spend more of their lives sitting in one place than most adults do. This can induce a sense of tiredness and can affect their learning. Secondly, young children *need* to move – it is through physical movement and contact that they develop a fuller experience of the world. It is entirely natural that children are far more "physical" than adults – that is part of the way they learn. In language learning, we can harness this to help learning become "deeper" and more memorable for the children.

Practical ideas

- If the children have already been sitting at their desks for a long time, start the lesson with some physical activity – perhaps an activity where they have to do what "Simon says" (see "Games" in *Extra activities*), or a song with actions.
- If you want children to **act out** a story, encourage them to include action in it that is, not just saying the words, but moving arms and legs, making gestures, miming actions, etc.
- If the children are repeating some words after you, make an action which they can copy while they say the word. With some words, the action will be obvious (for example, for *house* draw a roof and walls in the air). For other words there won't be an obvious action, but it is still useful to make some gesture. You can then repeat the gestures as a way of getting the children to remember and say the words.
- Mime is also a useful way to include physical action. If a child mimes a series of actions, perhaps ones that come from one of the stories in the course, the other children can say the words that go with the actions.

A–Z: teaching young learners

Picture dictionary

What and why?
American English Primary Colors includes six *Picture Dictionary* pages in the Activity Book. These make use of stickers to build a "dictionary" from the vocabulary that the children have learned.

Practical ideas
- It is probably best if the *Picture Dictionary* pages are completed in class, especially at the beginning of the course. This will help you to make sure that it is completed correctly and that the stickers are not stuck somewhere else!
- Before the children stick the pictures into the dictionary pages, make sure that they know exactly where they should go. Ask the children to put their finger on the place where they will stick the picture, and go around the class to check.
- You can use the dictionaries to play "I spy" (see "Games" in *Extra activities*). When the children have completed a few *Picture Dictionary* pages, ask them to find something beginning with a particular letter, or from clues, for example, *Find a fruit that is yellow.*
- You can play "Bingo" (see "Games" in *Extra activities*). Ask the children to choose six items from a *Picture Dictionary* page. They write the words in the squares on their "Bingo" board and close their books. You then call out words from the *Picture Dictionary* page in random order. You can make this more challenging if you say the meaning in the mother tongue, show a picture or give a clue, rather than saying the word itself.
- The children can play "Guess what?" in pairs. Choose a *Picture Dictionary* page and, with the children, make up some questions about each object. For example: *Can you eat it? Is it yellow? Is it big? Can you live in it?* The children then sit in pairs. One child thinks of one of the pictures, and the other child has to ask questions to guess what it is.

Previewing

What and why?
Most young children are easily distracted. This means that in the course of a lesson they can easily lose track of where they are and forget what they are doing. This can lead to problems not only for themselves, but also for other children if they start to disturb the class. Similarly, unless they are told clearly what they are going to do, it is often difficult for them to see the point or understand how they should be working. One way of trying to make sure that all the children are following the lesson is to start by previewing what they are going to do.

Practical ideas
- One way of previewing is to tell the children what they will be doing in the lesson. For example, *Today, Jess and Nick are in the balloon, but they have an accident!* You can also tell them what they will learn. For example, *Today, you can learn how to talk about what you can do.*
- Telling them works with some children, but for many others it can go in one ear and out the other! For *all* children, what is more important is *doing something*. You can get the children to preview, for example, by asking them to look for things in the coming pages, by looking for particular exercises (e.g. an exercise with a CD symbol, an exercise where they will work in pairs, etc.).
- You can put your plan for the coming lessons on a poster and stick it on the wall. Some children can draw suitable pictures beside activities on the poster – for example singing a song, making a bookmark, doing an exercise in the Activity Book. When **starting a lesson**, you can point to the things they will be doing that lesson.
- You can preview at the beginning of a week, at the beginning of a lesson, and – if there are many steps involved (e.g. in a **Story** section) – before the children start an activity.

A–Z: teaching young learners

Self-assessment

What and why?

In order to learn effectively, we all need to have a clear idea of our strengths and weaknesses. This helps us to know when we need more practice, and when we need to ask for help. Many learners unfortunately never really develop a clear idea of why they get the marks they do at school – it seems that "a mark" comes from some black box that the teacher chooses from at random. It is important, therefore, that we help children to develop an idea of what they have been learning, and how well they think they have done. At these early stages, the emphasis in self-assessment must be on developing the children's sense of competence. This is an important element in **motivation**.

Practical ideas

- The *Review* sections in the Activity Book include an "I can ..." section. This is intended to show the children what they have learned – that is, what they can do. It is important to create a sense of achievement in this. After asking for examples of things they can say, *everybody* should color in the star, regardless of how well you think they really know it. A sense of success is vitally important early on.

- If children are not doing very well, rather than giving them a sense of failure, ask them how they think they can improve. (This can realistically only be done in the mother tongue.) Discuss with them what they find difficult, and make suggestions of things that you and they can do to help them improve.

- Positive self-esteem in learning is an important element in continued success. At the end of each week or month, you could ask the children what they think they have learned. You could make a poster of *Things we can say in English* to put on the wall.

- Some children start to lose self-confidence very early in their school life, and it can take years to restore it. Teachers need to be sensitive to the children's view of themselves, and to give encouragement and support if they are developing a poor image of themselves as learners. Praise effort as well as actual achievement.

Songs and chants

What and why?

The songs and chants on the *Songs and Stories* CD have been written specifically for the course. They give the children more listening practice as well as help them practice new structures and vocabulary in a memorable and meaningful context. Once the children have learnt a new song or chant, it is a good idea to repeat it as an introductory or closing activity for the next few units.

Practical ideas

- You could ask the children to make a "shaker" in one of your first lessons with them – see *Extra activities*, page T83 in the Teacher's Book. The shaker, a cardboard tube filled with dried beans, can be used each time they are learning or singing a song. They shake the shaker to provide rhythm and this helps them to learn the melody of the song or chant. For apprehensive or shy children, the shaker can offer security.

- Some children are not naturally musical or perhaps are slightly deaf. They may respond better to being allowed to hum or "la la" the tune to help them learn the melody and can then add the words later.

- When the children know a song or chant, ask them to work in pairs to sing/chant it together – perhaps taking one alternate line each. If they want to, some pairs can then perform the song or chant in front of the class.

- For many songs and chants children can work in pairs facing each other. They can clap their own hands to the rhythm, then clap right hand to right hand and left hand to left hand with their partner.

- Children often like to sing or chant when they are standing in a line with their hands on the waist or shoulders of the person in front of them. This helps them learn the rhythm and any movements involved.

- Where possible, you can encourage the children to make up new words for the song or chant.

A–Z: teaching young learners

Special needs

What and why?
All children are "special," of course, and every child has needs which teachers need to take into account. The phrase *special needs*, however, is normally used to refer to children who have particular teaching/learning needs, most commonly children who are disadvantaged in "normal" classroom procedures. In many cases, children with special needs are identified by the school system and extra support is provided. Often, however, the difficulties that a child suffers may go unnoticed until it is too late. These may include partial deafness, limited vision, reading difficulties, restlessness, hyperactivity, and so on. English teachers are not normally qualified to make judgements about the special needs of a child, and should resist making statements about their capabilities. In common with other teachers, however, an English teacher can have a role in identifying a child who is in need of extra help or attention.

Practical ideas
- Try to view each child in your class as an individual. Take time to focus specifically on each child for brief periods and notice what difficulties they appear to be having.
- If a child is having problems keeping up or understanding, try to find out why. Talk to the child and see if he/she has problems hearing or seeing the board. Ask if he or she would like to move nearer the front of the class, or away from sources of noise such as a noisy corridor or a fan.
- Children who are disruptive in the classroom or who create other **discipline** problems may be in need of some extra attention and support. Sometimes, for example, they may misbehave because they are avoiding problems with reading or writing.
- If you do identify a child who you think is in need of extra help, try to talk to a specialist and hear their opinion. You may also talk to the parents. This needs to be done very sensitively, however, to avoid causing any extra anxiety.
- Finally, it is important not to lay the blame for failure on the child. Many children do need extra help, but equally, many come to be labeled "special needs children" because of failings in the classroom.

Starting a lesson

What and why?
Many things happen at the beginning of a lesson which, as teachers, we may be unaware of. The first moments of a lesson can establish for a child how far they feel "included" and whether they will understand what is happening. Many things are happening in a child's life, and to expect them to suddenly "switch into" an English lesson without being "eased in" will often mean that some children don't make the transition until too late – sometimes not until the lesson is ending! It may be some days since their last English lesson, or they may have just been involved in some very different activity (another subject, a game, playtime, etc.). It is important, then, to "build a bridge" into the English lesson.

Practical ideas
- You can play some music as they come into the class or as you get things ready – for example, play one of the songs that they know.
- You can start with "a round" – that is, going around the class. Everyone can say something that they remember from the last lesson: a word, a song, something that happened, a spelling – anything. If they don't know what to say, they can just say *I learned some English!*
- Instead of a round, you can ask the children to "brainstorm" in groups, noting down things that happened or that they remember. You can ask each group for one or two of the things that they remember.
- You can achieve the same thing with a quiz. Ask the children to look back at the pages they have covered in the book and find certain things, for example, particular words, what a person was

wearing, how many people were in a picture, and so on.
- "Show and tell" is a good way to start a lesson, making the children feel personally involved. You could ask them to bring in something that has something to do with English – for example, some English that they have found on a packet, a postcard they have received, a book in English that they have at home, etc.

Stories

What and why?

Stories provide an ideal focus and context for English, and at the same time serve to broaden the children's view of the world and their place in it. Firstly, the language of the story is presented in a recognizable situation and allows for the natural recycling of language. Secondly, stories provide an excellent opportunity for extensive listening. The ability to sit still and listen to a story is a skill which can be transferred from the mother tongue but, for many children, this takes time and practice to learn. Thirdly, stories allow children to identify with the characters and setting through visual clues which combine fantasy and reality. This allows them to develop their own understanding of narrative, and thereby brings about deeper learning.

Practical ideas

- At the beginning, the children are more likely to become involved in a story if you tell it first. Prepare the story beforehand by listening to the CD a few times until you are familiar with the words and intonation. You may want to select some of the Vocabulary Cards or put some other key words and phrases on cards, so that you can hold them up or stick them to the board or wall while you are telling the story.
- If possible, ask the children to sit in a circle around you – on chairs or on the floor – while you are telling the story. This change of position will put the children in the frame of mind for a story and will also make sure that they can all see your expressions and hear your voice clearly.
- Before telling a story, ask the children to look closely at the pictures so they can get a rough idea of what happens. Then ask them to close their books and listen without looking at the pictures.
- When you have told the story once without books, ask a few questions in the mother tongue to check that the children have understood. These can be "open" rather than "closed" questions, to allow children the opportunity to think of individual responses. Closed questions are usually about facts, for example, *Where is the man?* or *What is the dog's name?* Open questions ask children how they feel or respond, for example, *Would you like to be in a jungle? What would you do if you found a magic hat?*
- Tell the story again, and in order to allow for participation, encourage the children to say the sentences or phrases that are repeated in the story with you. You can do this by miming, pointing, and saying the phrase slowly.
- When you play the recording, ask children to volunteer to mime each of the roles in the story.
- At the end of the story, children can **act it out**. Some children prefer to learn some lines by heart and say them to each other in pairs or small groups. Others will prefer to do this as a performance. Here it is useful to use masks, hats, or other dress-up items to help them get into character.

A–Z: teaching young learners

Teacher exhaustion

What and why?

It is a common experience of many teachers that they end the teaching semester, week, or even day, absolutely exhausted. While "overworking" may be necessary from time to time, and may produce feelings of achievement, it is equally true that, in the long run, exhausted teachers are of little use to anyone – themselves, their immediate family, or the class they are teaching. Stress levels are often very high in the teaching profession. It is important to identify where the stress is coming from – is it from institutional structure (the school and school system), from the classroom (the particular class you have now) or from other factors?

Practical ideas

- A golden rule for all teachers is to realize that "you can only do what you can do." Many of the things that frustrate and stress teachers are beyond their control. Additionally, there are only a certain number of working hours in a day, and this places limits on what can be achieved. It is important, therefore, to be realistic, to do what you can and not to blame yourself for achieving less than you hoped.
- Stress can result from teaching a particular class of children. This may be lessened by alternative approaches in your relationship with them. See **Discipline**.
- Many teachers simply work too hard, and do not realize that, in many cases, the more they do, the less the children may benefit. A teacher, for example, may sit up all night preparing a craft activity for the children, or even making the item completely for them, and not realize that by doing this they are robbing the children of the experience of doing things for themselves. A craft item made completely by a child is unlikely to look as nice as one made, for the most part by an adult, but in the end, what is more important – the child's experience or the finished article?
- "Over-preparing" is also common. It is possible to involve children in many of the things that teachers traditionally do by themselves. This may be organizing materials, preparing the classroom, planning tasks, even designing simple practice exercises and simple tests. See **Mixed abilities**.
- Exhaustion can also come about by assuming too much responsibility – often to the detriment of the children. A teacher who asks *How can I make the children speak English when they are in groups?*, for example, is probably asking the wrong question. The emphasis on how *I* can resolve the problem, and how I can *make* them do something puts the teacher in a "compulsion" relationship with the children which in all likelihood they will resist – thereby creating another problem. A more fruitful approach is to share the problem with the children and say *Our group work isn't working. How can we improve it?*
- Similarly, some teachers feel that they have to find ways of *motivating* the children when they seem to be losing interest. This places the teacher in the role of continually looking for "fun" things to do to "sugar the pill" and seemingly trying to get the children to learn despite themselves. In many cases, the real issue is not of finding ways to "motivate" the children but of finding ways to develop the children's *own* motivation. See **Motivation**.

Extra activities

Games

Games are an active and enjoyable way for children to use new language and build up confidence. It is important that any games you use really do involve using language, and that the time you spend on the game benefits all the children. Some games, therefore, are best avoided, because although they may involve the use of English, it will only be at a very minimal level – the game "Hangman" is an example.

Here are some general notes on using games.

1 **Before starting a game,** it is important that all the children know exactly what they have to do. If you can, explain this in the mother tongue and get the children to explain it back to you. The game itself is then played in English. Alternatively, before the children begin playing, get two or three of them to play a practice round in front of the class, so that everyone can see how it works.

2 **A successful classroom game is likely to be noisy!** You won't want to let things get out of hand, but it is important to allow the children the "space" to show their enthusiasm.

3 **Encourage the children to use English** while they are playing. Giving them suggested language to use will be very helpful. You could write the language on cards to hand out or on a poster to stick up on the wall.

4 **Don't let a game go on too long.** It is best to stop the game while the children are still enjoying it – that way, they will want to play it again. If you play some music during the game, the end of the music can signal a natural end to the game.

5 **Use games at different points in a lesson,** not only at the end – otherwise, children can begin to see a game as a "reward." In many ways, a game can be just as serious and important as any other classroom activity.

6 **Keep everybody involved.** Games in which more and more children are "out" (i.e. drop out of the game when they make a mistake) may be a lot of fun for the winner, but can be demoralizing for the others, as well as wasting their time. After all, it is the weaker students who need more practice. It is best, then, to avoid games which gradually eliminate children from the game.

7 **A game is a good opportunity for you to use English naturally.** Example phrases:

Let's play a game.
Do you want to play a game?
Make a circle.
Make two teams.
Sit on the floor.
Move your chairs over here.
Who wants to start?
Who would like to be in the middle?
Who wants to be the team leader?
Find a partner.
Face your partner.
Play in / Get into groups of four.
Take turns.
Whose turn is it?
Ready, set, go!

The following are some suggestions for games that work well with young children.

Action game

The children sit in a circle. Go round giving every child a number: *You're number 1, you're number 2 ...* up to 10 – then continue from number 1 again. This means that several children will have the same number – if you have a class of 30, for example, there will be three number 1s, three number 2s, etc. When you say a number, those children stand up and do/mime the action that you give them. For example: *One: jump! Two: clap! Three: hop! Four: click! Five: sing! Six: count! Seven: wave! Eight: dance! Nine: draw! Ten: walk!*

Alphabet game

Children sit or stand in a circle facing inwards. Give each child a letter of the alphabet: *You are A, you are B ...*, etc. Stand in the middle of the circle and say two letters, for example, C and T. These two children stand up and quickly trade places. If you have fewer than 26 children, give some children two letters. If you say both of their letters, they turn around instead of trading places with someone else.

VARIATION

You can say words instead of letters, for example, *cat* and *teacher*. The children with the first letter of each word (*c* and *t*) say their letter aloud and change places as before.

Extra activities

Alphabet squares

Children play in pairs. Each child draws a grid of 10 x 10 squares. The squares along the top are numbered 1–10 and those down the side have letters A–J. Children write all the letters of the alphabet randomly in the squares without their partner seeing what they are doing. The aim of the game is to "hit" as many as possible of their partner's squares which have a letter. For example, the children take turns saying *8F* or *6G*. If that square has a letter in it, the partner says, for example, *Yes, that's T*. The first child then has to write down a word *beginning with* or *containing* that letter, for example, *teacher* or *cat*. The child with the most words written down at the end of the game is the winner.

	1	2	3	4	5	6	7	8	9	10
A	F				P					
B			I	W				D		V
C		Q		A						
D				E				L		
E	R		B			M				U
F				N				Y	T	
G		G				C				
H				O						
I	H		J		X			K		
J			S							Z

Bingo

"Bingo" can be played very simply by asking children to draw their own boards – a grid with six or eight squares. They then write words, letters, numbers, or draw pictures in each square. They can use torn pieces of paper to cover the squares when they hear their items called.

"Bingo" is an old favorite, and many children absolutely love it. However, it has limited value, and should not be overused – even if the children request it again and again! The key point is to make sure that the game includes an emphasis on *meaning*. If, for example, the children each have a board with words written on it and their only task is to listen for those words, then the game is literally *meaningless* and probably not worth doing. You can make sure that there is a focus on meaning if you adapt the game in different ways, for example:

1. Say the words in the mother tongue and the children have to find the English words on their board; or vice versa.
2. Hold up pictures and they have to look for the words.
3. Say things related in meaning to the words on their boards – for example, opposites or definitions.

Circle word game

This game recycles new vocabulary. The children sit in a circle with you. You will need a small ball. Start the game by saying a word, and throw the ball to a child. The child says a related word (or if they can't think of one, they can say the same word) and then throws the ball to someone else. The ball should move quite quickly.

VARIATION

To make the game more demanding, you can ask the children to make a sentence with the word that is "thrown" to them. As before, they then say a new word before throwing the ball to someone else. If a child can't make a sentence, allow him/her to just say a word.

Find and show (classroom objects)

Children work in teams of six. Write the names of classroom objects on the board with the letters mixed up. For example, instead of writing *marker*, write *kmrrae*. The children work out what the word is and the first team to bring the object to the desk gets a point.

I spy (I can see ...)

In this game, you supply a clue about an object that you can see, and the children have to make suggestions until they identify it. You can make various decisions about:

- where the object is (in the classroom, outside the window, on a page in their book).
- how you give the clues (for example, *I spy ... something beginning with B / something yellow / something that we can eat / something long / something that grows on trees*).

VARIATIONS

- You can give the clues in the mother tongue, but only accept an answer in English.

Extra activities

- You can write a list of clues on the board. The children race each other in teams to find the objects.
- The children can make similar "I spy" races for each other.
- You can use the game to familiarize the children with what they will be doing in the coming units in the book. Make a list of things they must search for in the pages.

Kim's game

This is a memory game. If you have a small class, you can play the game with the whole group. If the class is large (20+), organize groups of six. Put eight items on the table (a ruler, a pencil, etc.) and allow one minute for the children to look at them. Cover the items with a cloth. Tell the children to close their eyes, and then remove one item from the table and hide it. Uncover the table and ask them to work out which item is missing. When they get the right answer, replace the item and cover the table again. The child who answered correctly can take your place and remove an item, and so the game continues.

VARIATIONS

- Instead of objects, you can use Vocabulary Cards.
- Instead of removing an item, you can simply move it to another position on the table. The children have to say which item has moved.
- When you remove an item and uncover the table, the children write down the missing item without saying anything. Re-cover the table and slip the item back under the cloth. Then repeat the procedure a few times, with the children writing down the item that is missing each time you uncover the table. At the end, ask children to read out their lists and, finally, supply the correct answers.

The name game

For this game, divide the class into pairs of teams to play against each other (four children per team is ideal). In each team, the children choose names for themselves (one name for each child in the group). All the names they choose must be related. For example, they might be names of cartoon characters, sports people, cities, or teachers at their school. For students who know more English, the names could be of things, for example, names of items in a classroom, names of food items, and so on.

Team A writes the first letter of each of their names on the board. Team B then asks one of them *What's your name?*, and that person must answer (*My name's ...*). By looking at the letters on the board and asking one or two questions, the children in Team B try to guess each of the other related names. They win a point for each name they guess correctly.

The number game

The children are sitting down. Give out "badges" with different numbers on them (1 to 10, or 1 to 20, depending on what the children have learned). Say the numbers in random order. When you say the number on their badge, the children stand up. Then say the numbers again in a different order. When you say the number that follows theirs, they sit down.

Simon says

This is a very well-known game. The children have to follow your instructions to do something, but *only* instructions that start with the words *Simon says* (for example, *Simon says stand up*). If you don't say *Simon says*, they should ignore the instruction. Anyone who makes a mistake can have a sticker stuck on them (this is better than telling them to drop out of the game). The person who has the fewest stickers at the end is the winner.

VARIATIONS

- You can replace *Simon says ...* with *King Cat says ...* to provide a link with the course.
- You can play one of the songs on the CD during the game, to provide a time limit.
- You can make the game more complex by asking the children to follow the previous instruction. In this case, don't use the words *Simon says* at all. For example:
  Sit down. (Children do nothing.)
  Stand up. (Children sit down.)
  Clap your hands. (Children stand up.)
- After you have given an example, the children can play the game in small groups.

Treasure hunt

This game is suitable if you have space for the children to move around and a group that is not too big. If you have many different things/areas in your classroom you can play it inside, otherwise it should be done in a bigger area.

Extra activities

On small pieces of paper, write clues and hide them. The clues link to each other, so that by working out the answer to one clue the children know where they have to look for their next one. Some clues might ask them to work something out – they bring their answer to you and you give them the next clue. A sequence of about ten clues is usually enough. If you divide the class into groups, you can write the clues on different colored papers (a different color for each group) and hide the same clues in a different sequence for each group. In this case, the children must be told that if they find a clue for another group, they must not touch it.

At the end, each group has to bring all the clues to you, in the correct order with the correct answers. It is a good idea to have a prize for everyone so there are no losers (this can be something small such as a pencil or eraser).

The following are some examples of clues for a classroom treasure hunt. Each clue indicates where the children should look for the next one. The clues you use will need to be adapted for your classroom.

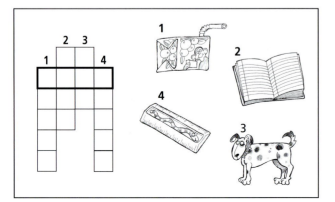

Crafts

Craft activities have a very useful role to play in the classroom. They personalize the English classes, physically involve the children, give them "space" and make learning more memorable. See **A–Z Craft activities** for more information. The Storytime sections in each unit include craft activities, but here are some more simple activities which you may like to use.

Greetings cards

The children can make greetings cards at virtually any time of the year. Some possibilities are:

Mother's Day
Father's Day
Christmas
spring/summer/autumn/winter
turning the clock back/forward
birthdays
Easter
Halloween
illness
retirement
moving away
getting married
passing an exam

The children can make greetings cards by taking a piece of card or stiff paper and folding it in half. They can decorate the front and inside with their own designs.

They could also cut a small "window" in the front of the card and glue something in the window from the back, such as a piece of patterned material, some nice paper, a photograph or a picture they have made. They could also scribble on another piece of paper with water-based markers, spray it lightly with water so that the color runs, and leave it to dry. The resulting blurred colors can be very attractive and unusual and look nice in the card "window." Another piece of paper can be stuck on the back of the window, to cover the back of the design.

The children can then write a message on the front or inside:

Happy birthday!
Happy Christmas/Easter!
Happy summer holidays!
Congratulations!
Goodbye ... we will miss you!
To a very special person
Get well soon
To the best Mom/Dad in the world
Season's greetings
Good luck with your new house/job

Animal ears

The children can make cat and dog ears to wear on their heads. These can be great fun, especially when they are acting as Kip or King Cat. You can photocopy the instructions and the cut-out for the ears on page T84. The children will need:

- 1 strip of stiff paper 55 x 10 cm for the headband.
- 2 pieces of stiff paper 18 x 18 cm for the ears. Pencil, scissors, stapler, or glue stick.
- Markers to color and decorate.
- Face paints.

Bookmarks

Welcome! A in the Activity Book shows the children how they can make a bookmark in the shape of a balloon. There are many more similar designs that you can use, which clip over the pages in a similar way. You can photocopy one of the cut-outs on pages T85–T88 for the children to color in. After each lesson, the children could write some of the words that they have learned on the bookmark.

Extra activities

Paper bangers

See instructions and photos on page T89. A paper banger is a lot of fun – but it can be noisy! It is made from newspaper and makes a loud bang when you move it quickly down through the air. The children could use paper bangers when they are acting the stories in the Student's Book – for example, when the balloon crashes into the house (Unit 2A), when the birds attack the balloon (Unit 4A), when the balloon crashes into the tree (Unit 4C), when Taffy bites the car tire (Unit 4D), and when the wave crashes onto the balloon (Unit 5A).

Secret writing

Children love secret writing – or invisible ink. They can write messages in English which they can take home to their family. If they make a rounded, blunt point out of a matchstick or toothpick they can use it as a "pen." You can make invisible ink with potato juice, milk, lemon juice, or onion juice. The message will only show clearly when the paper is warmed gently, for example under a hair dryer or on a very warm surface (e.g. a classroom radiator).

Shakers

Shakers can be good to use with songs and chants. A shaker is a cardboard tube, closed at one end with a circle of cardboard, filled with small stones or dried beans and then sealed at the other end with a small circle of cardboard. The shaker can then be decorated by each child and used each time they are learning or singing a song. They shake the shaker to provide rhythm, and this helps them learn the melody of the song or chant.

Animal ears

You will need:
1 strip of stiff paper 55 x 10 cm (headband)
2 pieces of stiff paper 18 x 18 cm for the ears
pencil, scissors, stapler/glue stick
markers to color and decorate
face paint

DOG EARS
1. Copy the template twice. Cut out the ears.
2. Decorate the ears and headband.
3. Staple the ears to the headband so that they hang down.
4. Put it on. Paint your face!

CAT EARS
1. Copy the template twice. Cut out the ears.
2. Decorate the ears and headband with markers.
3. Staple the ears onto the headband.
4. Put it on. Paint your face!

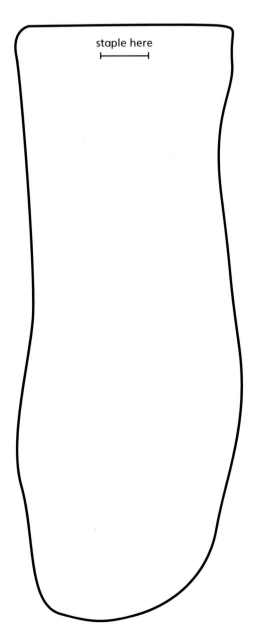

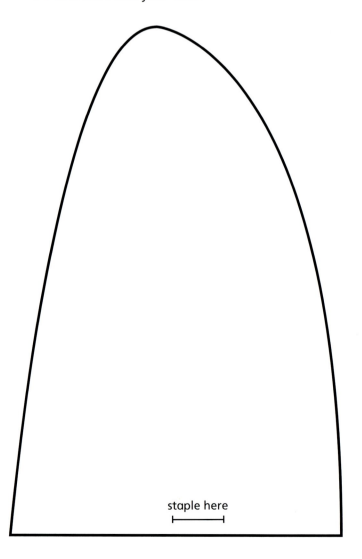

Elephant bookmark

Face bookmark

Octopus bookmark

Rocket bookmark

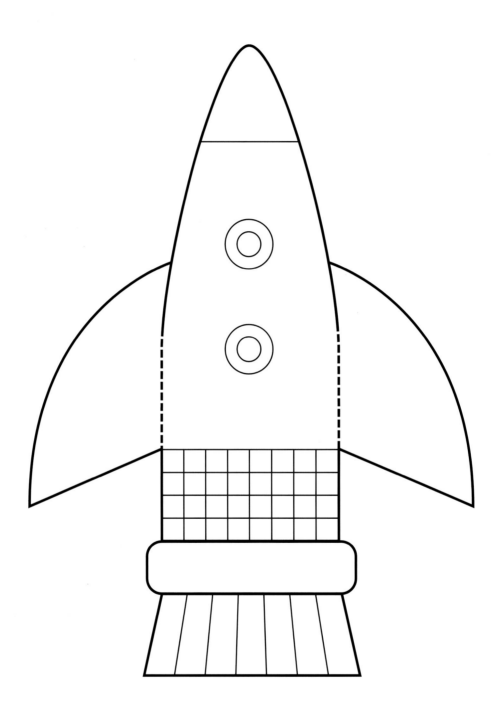

Paper banger
Instructions

1 Fold the paper. Open it.

2 Fold the corners.

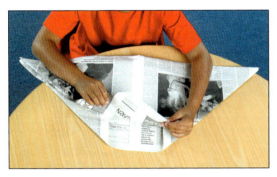
3 Fold the paper in half.

4 Fold the paper. Open it.

5 Fold the corners.

6 Turn the paper over. Fold it in half.

7 Hold the paper. Move it quickly.

8 You can paint it and write on it.

Unit 1 Extra practice

1 Write your answers.

a Six and three are ..... nine .....   **e** Five and three are ....

b Four and six are ....   **f** Six and one are ....

c Two and seven are ....   **g** Four and two are ....

d One and one are ....   **h** Three and one are ....

2 Count and write.

a
Six bananas

b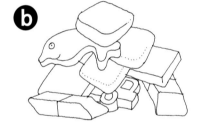

c

d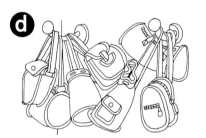

e

f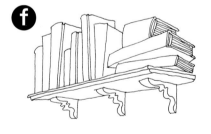

g

h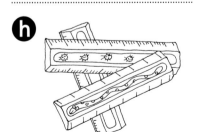

i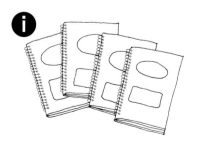

3 Complete the sentences.

What's this?
It's a sweet.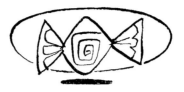

What's that?
.... sandwich.

What's this?
....

What's .... ?
....

What's .... ?
....

4 Match the sentences to the pictures.

1. Bananas are my favorite fruit.
2. Milk is my favorite drink.
3. Chocolate cake is my favorite cake.
4. *Storytime* is my favorite TV program.

Unit 2 Extra practice

1 Draw lines.

Tomas Sally Vincent

Susi David Pam

This is Tomas.   He's ten.

This is Sally.   He's eleven.

This is Vincent.   He's thirteen.

This is Susi.   She's eleven.

This is David.   She's twelve.

This is Pam.   She's eight.

2 Think! Write the next numbers.

two   four   six   eight   ...ten...   twelve   ....

three   six   nine   ....

five   ....   fifteen

three   seven   eleven   ....

one   five   nine   ....

3 Read about Joanne's classroom. Draw lines.

That's my bag.

That's my desk.

This is Jess. She's my friend.

This is my classroom. It's big.

This is Mrs. Dell. She's my teacher.

4 Draw a picture of your classroom. Write about it.

This is _____

That's _____

This is _____

He's/She's _____

This is _____

He's/She's _____

Unit 3 Extra practice

1 Draw six more lines. Draw the pictures. Color.

four	six	nine	seven	three	two	five
red	yellow	blue	green	white	black	brown
pens	cars	houses	cats	dogs	balls	bananas

2 Correct the sentences.

Look! Two cats!
They aren't cats.
They're dogs.

Look! A pen!
It isn't

Look! Three balls!

Look! Three dogs!

Look! A cat!

Look! A ruler!

3 Look at the pictures. Read the sentences and check the box.

                              Picture A   Picture B

1 There are two dogs. ☐ ☐
2 There is a small car. ☐ ☐
3 There are five cats. ☐ ☐
4 There are six balls. ☐ ☐

Picture A

Picture B

4 Find three more differences. Write about them.

In Picture A, there _____

but in Picture B, there _____

In Picture A, _____

but in Picture B, _____

In Picture A, _____

but _____

Unit 4 Extra practice

1 Write the names of the animals.

1. cow
2. ....
3. ....
4. ....
5. ....
6. ....
7. ....
8. ....
9. ....

2 Write the missing numbers and words.

| 11 | .... | 13 | 14 | .... |
| .... | twelve | thirteen | .... | fifteen |

| 16 | 17 | 18 | 19 | 20 |
| sixteen | .... | eighteen | .... | .... |

Write the answer.

Nine and nine are ....   Eleven and six are ....

Fourteen and five are ....   Sixteen and four are ....

Six and seven are ....   Ten and three are ....

3. Read about a kangaroo. Choose the correct word.

This is a kangaroo.
Kangaroos are from
Australia / Africa.
They are grey and red / green.
They can swim / jump very fast.

4. Look at the pictures. Write about tigers and zebras.

This is ....
Tigers ....
....
They are yellow/orange
and ....
Tigers can ....

This is a zebra. Zebras ...

Unit 5 Extra practice

1 Label the face.

head

2 Read and draw lines. Write the name.

It has small eyes and a big mouth.

It has short hair and big eyes.

It has big ears and small eyes.

It has long hair and big ears.

It has small eyes and a small mouth.

It has a long nose and big eyes.

shark

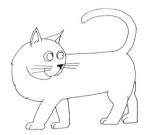

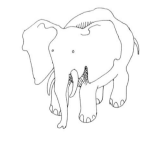

3 Follow the lines. Write what they have.

Maria   Sam   Steve   Nadia   Daniel   Sue

Daniel: He has

Steve:

Nadia:

Sue:

Maria and Sam:

4 Find out where the animals live and what they eat. Write about them!

Pandas

Hippos

Unit 6 Extra practice

1 Does Sam have everything? Check the box.

Ice cream ☐
Milk ☐
Cheese ☐
Apples ☐
Oranges ☐
Fish ☐
....
....
....
....
....

2 Write the extra things on Sam's list.

3 Write the days of the week.

On Mondays, I go swimming.
On _Tuesdays_, I do my homework at home.
On ...., I play soccer in the park.
On ...., go to my friend's house.
On ...., I watch my favorite program on TV.
On .... and ...., I play with my friends.

4) Read Exercise 3 again. Write the day for each picture.

a .... b .... c .... d ....

e .... f .... and ....

5) Look at the pictures. Write Sue's words.

On Mondays and Wednesdays, I *do my homework at home.*
On Tuesdays, ...
On ....
On ....
On ....
On ....

Monday   Tuesday   Wednesday   Thursday

Friday   Saturday   Sunday

Tests

Introduction

At this level, you may well feel that testing is unnecessary and it certainly should not be a prominent feature of the course. The aim is to promote the children's enjoyment learning English, not to set up hurdles that may make them nervous, impair their confidence, or give them a feeling of failure. If you do choose to use any or all of the tests provided here, handle them lightly and give the children plenty of reassurance and support.

There are two main purposes for the tests. The first is to tell you how much the children have learned. The second is to tell you how effective your lessons are. There are many reasons why children succeed or fail in language learning, and consistently low scores in tests may indicate either that the individual child needs help or that the overall classroom experience is not very profitable. In the latter case, you may need to ask yourself why. The *A–Z: teaching young learners* will give you many ideas. It is important not to blame the children for failure.

Content of the tests

For every unit, there is a photocopiable test which should take about 25 minutes to complete. Each one contains five exercises based on the material presented in the Student's Book and involve a variety of skills. Two of these are listening exercises with scripts that you will need to dictate. In all exercises, the first answer is completed as an example.

Note: the children will need colored pencils or markers for Unit 3 Exercise 3 and Unit 5 Exercise 3.

General approach

We recommend the following approaches when using the tests:

- Give a test only when you feel that the class is thoroughly at home with the material in the unit.

- Present the test in a relaxed way, so that children see it as an extension of their normal class and homework activities, not as something "special" or more weighty. Assure them that the test is meant to allow them to show how much they know, not to trip them up.

- Make it clear beforehand what is going to be covered in the test and give the children time to prepare.

- Introduce the lesson with a short warm-up activity to get the children relaxed and focused on English. For example, you could hold up a selection of Vocabulary Cards and get them to say the words or to answer simple questions.

- Look at each exercise with the class before they start to answer and explain the task very clearly, using the mother tongue as well as the English instructions. Then do the example with them before they set to work on their own. Encourage them to ask questions and go over the explanation again if necessary.

- If the children seem worried or uncertain about an exercise, go through one or two more of the questions orally before they begin to write.

Listening exercises

The Listening material for the tests is not recorded – you will need to use the scripts on page T105. This is because the children will feel more relaxed when they hear your voice and also because you will have more control over the pace of the exercise. We suggest that you read each script aloud to the class three times, as follows:

1 Read the script through at a steady pace, while the children simply listen and look at the exercise.

2 Read it again at a slower speed, pausing after each question to give the children time to complete the task.

3 Read it through once more while the children check their answers.

Marking the tests

Each test carries a total of 30 marks. The Answer key is on page T104. You can collect the tests to mark yourself or, as a more informal procedure, you might allow the children to exchange papers and mark one another's work.

Interpreting scores

If all the children get over half the answers correct, you will know that the class is going well. If a few children get less than half the answers correct, you may need to spend extra time helping those individuals and giving them encouragement. If most of the children get less than half the answers correct, you will need to think about why this has happened and what changes might be necessary in your teaching.

Alternative ways of using the tests

- You could choose to break the tests into halves, giving you two shorter tests which can be completed quickly at the end or beginning of a lesson.

- If formal assessment through testing is not a priority, you might allow the children to work on the tests in pairs rather than completing them individually.

- If you don't want to test the children at all, you can use the test exercises as additional or alternative review material in class or for homework at the end of a unit.

Tests

Answer key

Unit 1

1. 2 no 3 yes 4 yes 5 no 6 no
2. 2 e 3 b 4 a 5 f 6 d
3. 3 erasers 6 pencil
   4 floor 7 ruler
   5 books
4. Students' drawings

Unit 2

1. 2 c 3 a 4 f 5 d 6 b
2. 2 No, it isn't.
   3 Yes, he is.
   4 No, she isn't.
   5 Yes, it is.
   6 Yes, she is.
3. 2 thirteen 5 six
   3 eleven 6 five
   4 fifteen
4. 2 a mouse. 5 isn't here.
   3 birthday. 6 our dog.
   4 is seven.

Unit 3

1. Joanne – car
   bears – garden
   cat – tree
   Zara – bus
   dogs – house
2. 2 f 3 a 4 b 5 e 6 c
3. Picture correctly colored
4. 2 There are 5 There are
   3 There's a 6 There's a
   4 There are

Unit 4

1. 2 b 3 a 4 b 5 b 6 a
2. 2 f 3 d 4 b 5 a 6 e
3. 2 eighteen 5 seventeen
   3 twenty 6 sixteen
   4 nineteen
4. 2 ✔ 3 ✘ 4 ✔ 5 ✘ 6 ✔

Unit 5

1. 2 d 3 f 4 a 5 e 6 c
2. 2 boy with big ears
   3 man with blond hair
   4 dog
   5 small boat
   6 fish in tank
3. Features correctly drawn and colored
4. 2 Tigers live in forests.
   3 Crocodiles eat animals.
   4 Horses eat grass.
   5 Fish live in the sea.
   6 Cows live on farms.

Unit 6

1. 2 b 3 a 4 b 5 b 6 a
2. Monday – a
   Wednesday – c
   Thursday – f
   Friday and Saturday – e
   Sunday – d
3. 2 no 3 yes 4 no 5 no 6 yes
4. 2 by car
   3 go swimming
   4 my homework
   5 watch TV
   6 play soccer

Tests

Scripts for Listening exercises

Unit 1

1 One. Is it a street?
Two. Is it a dog?
Three. Is it a house?
Four. Is it a car?
Five. Is it a school?
Six. Is it a bus?

2 One. Mmm, yummy! Bananas are very nice.
Two. Hello! My name's King Cat.
Three. What's that – is it a book? Oh no, it's a map.
Four. What's in my lunchbox? Let's see … A sandwich and a cupcake.
Five. Look! The balloon is up in the sky.
Six. Come on, let's go. Goodbye!

Unit 2

1 One. Hop.
Two. Jump.
Three. Clap.
Four. Stand up.
Five. Look at that house.
Six. Point to the door.

2 One. He's ten.
Two. The book is here.
Three. Nick is in the classroom.
Four. She's fifteen.
Five. It's a birthday party.
Six. Mrs. Dell is a teacher.

Unit 3

1 One. Jess and Nick are in the balloon.
Two. Joanne is in the car.
Three. There are two bears in the garden.
Four. There's a cat in the tree.
Five. Zara is in the bus.
Six. There are three dogs in the house.

2 One. She's cold.
Two. He's very strong.
Three. They're hot.
Four. It's small.
Five. They're big, but they aren't dangerous.
Six. Look – snow! It's very cold.

Unit 4

1 One. This is my Mom.
Two. My dog can swim.
Three. What's that? Oh, it's a cow.
Four. There are two hens in the garden.
Five. I can see a black bear.
Six. Look. There are three birds in the tree.

2 One. My name's Zara. I can jump high.
Two. Joanne can't run very fast.
Three. Tom can't fly.
Four. My name's Nick. I'm eight and I can read.
Five. That's Jess. She can climb trees.
Six. Kip is a dog. He can't write and he isn't very smart.

Unit 5

1 One. There's a tree house in our garden.
Two. There are ships in the sea.
Three. Look! It's an island.
Four. My friends live on a farm.
Five. There's a big river in my town.
Six. Let's walk in the forest.

2 One. I have two black cats.
Two. My brother has big ears.
Three. My Dad has blond hair.
Four. My dog has long hair.
Five. We have a boat, but it isn't very big.
Six. We have six small fish in our house.

Unit 6

1 One. I have an apple and a banana.
Two. Milk is a nice drink. I like it.
Three. There are three pears in my lunchbox.
Four. I don't like fish.
Five. I have a banana but I don't have an orange.
Six. I can see cupcakes and ice cream.

2 On Tuesdays I go to school by bike.
On Thursdays I play soccer with my friends.
On Sundays I do my homework.
On Wednesdays I go to school on foot.
On Mondays I go swimming after school.
On Fridays and Saturdays I watch TV.

Unit 1 test

Name _____   Class _____

1 Listen and circle your answer. (5 marks)

① yes no

② yes no

③ yes no

④ yes no

⑤ yes no

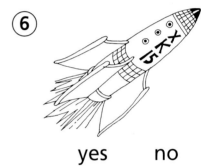
⑥ yes no

2 Listen and draw lines. (5 marks)

1
2
3
4
5
6

T106 © Cambridge University Press 2004 PHOTOCOPIABLE Unit 1 Test

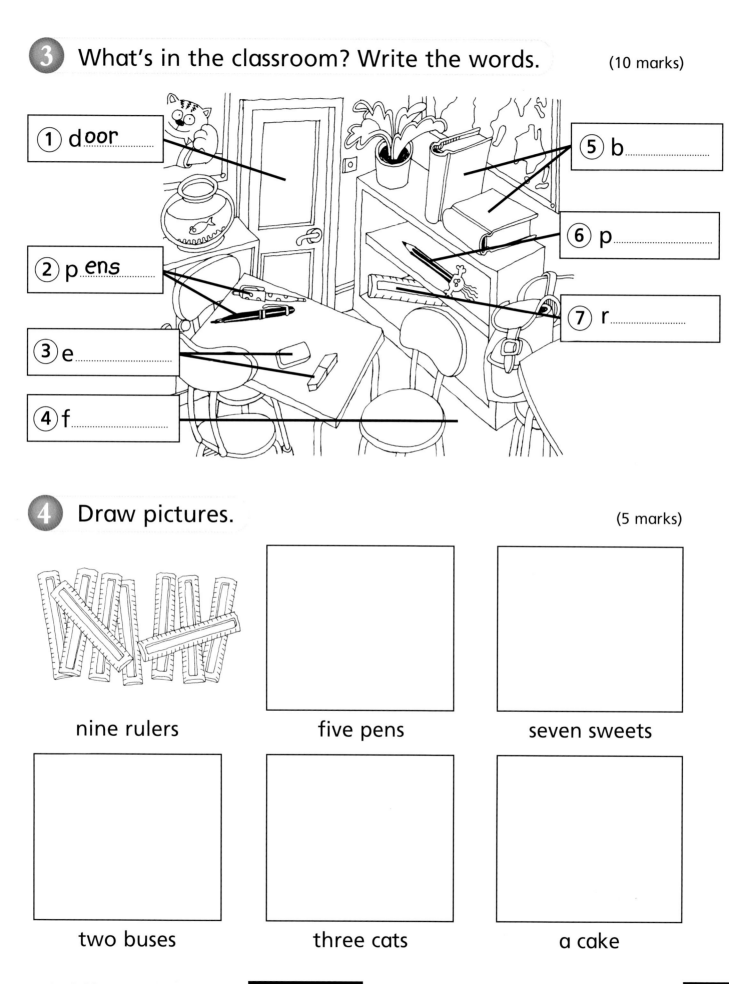

Unit 2 test

Name _____ Class _____

1 Listen and draw lines. (5 marks)

a    b    c

1
2
3
4
5
6

d   e   f

2 Listen and check (✓). (5 marks)

① Yes, he is. ☐
   No, he isn't. ✓

② Yes, it is. ☐
   No, it isn't. ☐

③ Yes, he is. ☐
   No, he isn't. ☐

④ Yes, she is. ☐
   No, she isn't. ☐

⑤ Yes, it is. ☐
   No, it isn't. ☐

⑥ Yes, she is. ☐
   No, she isn't. ☐

T108 © Cambridge University Press 2004 PHOTOCOPIABLE Unit 2 Test

3 Write the numbers. (10 marks)

1. Seven and three are __ten__.
2. Four and nine are _____.
3. Ten and one are _____.
4. Eight and seven are _____.
5. Six and _____ are twelve.
6. Nine and _____ are fourteen.

4 Draw lines. (5 marks)

①  ② 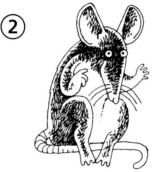 ③

④  ⑤  ⑥

1. Sam is   is seven.
2. Hello! I'm   our dog.
3. It's her   isn't here.
4. King Cat   my friend.
5. Karen   birthday.
6. Kip is   a mouse.

Unit 3 test

Name _____ Class _____

1 Where are they? Listen and draw lines. (5 marks)

2 Listen and write the numbers (1–6). (5 marks)

3 Color the picture. (5 marks)

4 Write *There's a* or *There are*. (10 marks)

1. **There's a** sandwich in my lunchbox.
2. .... five pens in my pencil case.
3. .... big tree in the garden.
4. .... two schools in this town.
5. .... twelve red balls here.
6. .... map in the car.

Unit 4 test

Name .... Class ....

1 Listen and circle a or b.   (5 marks)

2 Listen and draw lines.   (5 marks)

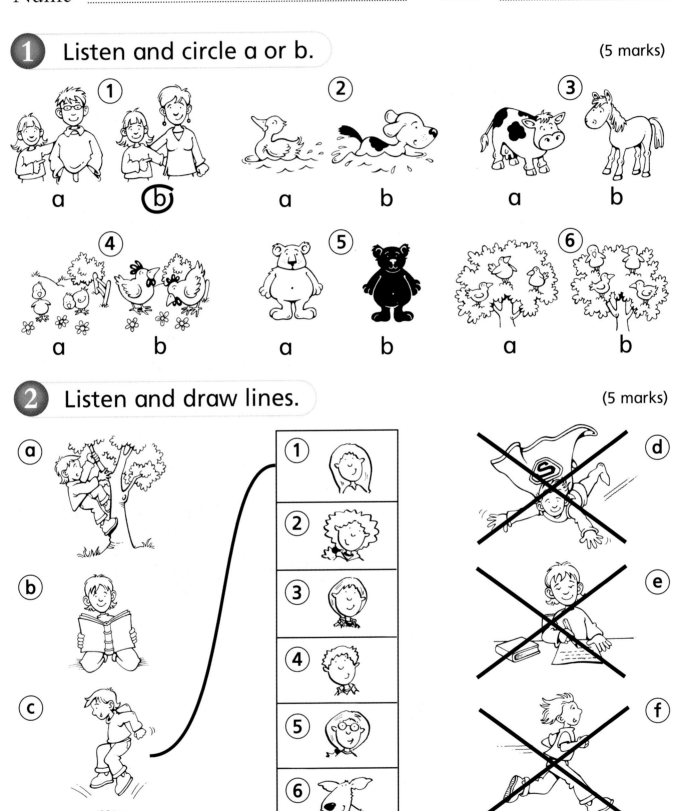

T112 © Cambridge University Press 2004   PHOTOCOPIABLE   Unit 4 Test

3. Count and write the numbers. (10 marks)

① twelve
dogs

② ....
cats

③ ....
birds

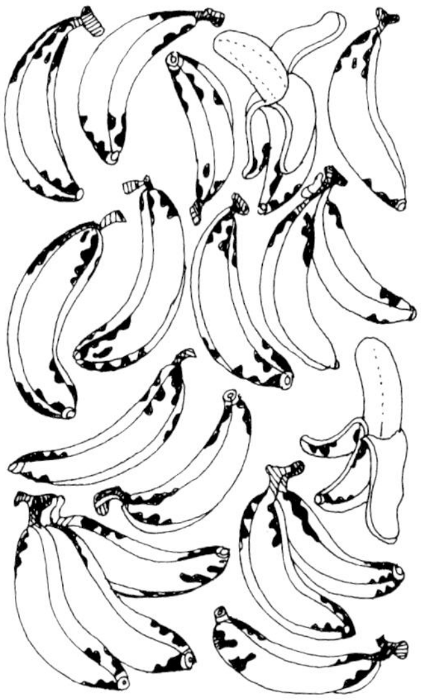

④ ....
bananas

⑤ ....
trees

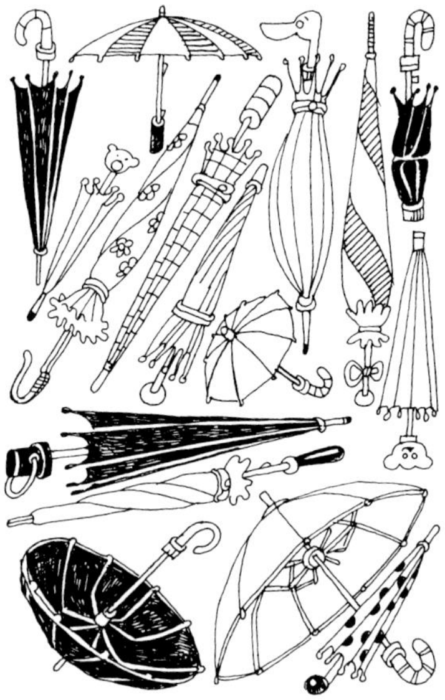

⑥ ....
umbrellas

4. Write ✓ or ✗. (10 marks)

(1) Cats can climb. ✓
(2) A chick is a small bird. ☐
(3) Dogs can't run. ☐
(4) An elephant is very big. ☐
(5) A hen can jump high. ☐
(6) Cows can't read and write. ☐

Unit 5 test

Name .... Class ....

1 Listen and write the numbers (1–6). (5 marks)

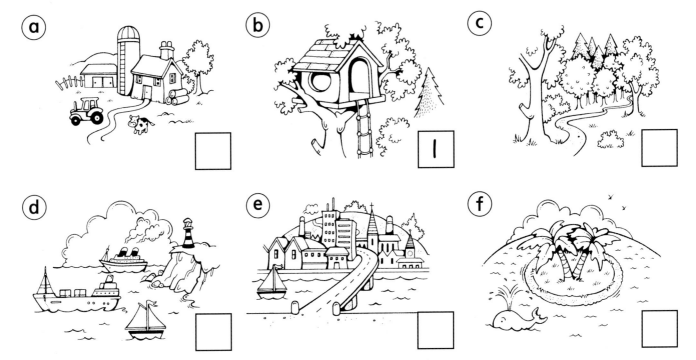

2 Listen and draw lines. (5 marks)

3 Draw and color. (5 marks)

This is my friend Eva.

She has short brown hair.

She has blue eyes.

She has a big mouth and a long nose.

4 Write sentences with *eat* or *live*. (10 marks)

1. Monkeys – fruit   Monkeys eat fruit.
2. Tigers – forests
3. Crocodiles – animals
4. Horses – grass
5. Fish – sea
6. Cows – farms

Unit 6 test

Name .... Class ....

1 Listen and circle a or b. (5 marks)

2 Listen and draw lines. (5 marks)

T116 © Cambridge University Press 2004 PHOTOCOPIABLE Unit 6 Test

3 Write *yes* or *no*. (5 marks)

1. Milk is a white drink. ......yes......
2. Tigers live in caves. ....
3. We can eat pears. ....
4. The next day after Wednesday is Tuesday. ....
5. Crocodiles like apples and oranges. ....
6. Ice cream is cold. ....

4 Look at the pictures. Write two words. (10 marks)

1. I go to school ...by... ...bus...

2. but I go home ....

3. I .... on Fridays.

4. I do .... after school.

5. I don't .... every day.

6. On Saturdays I .... in the park with my friends.

Templates

Balloon bookmark

Cut-out 1, Activity Book page 5

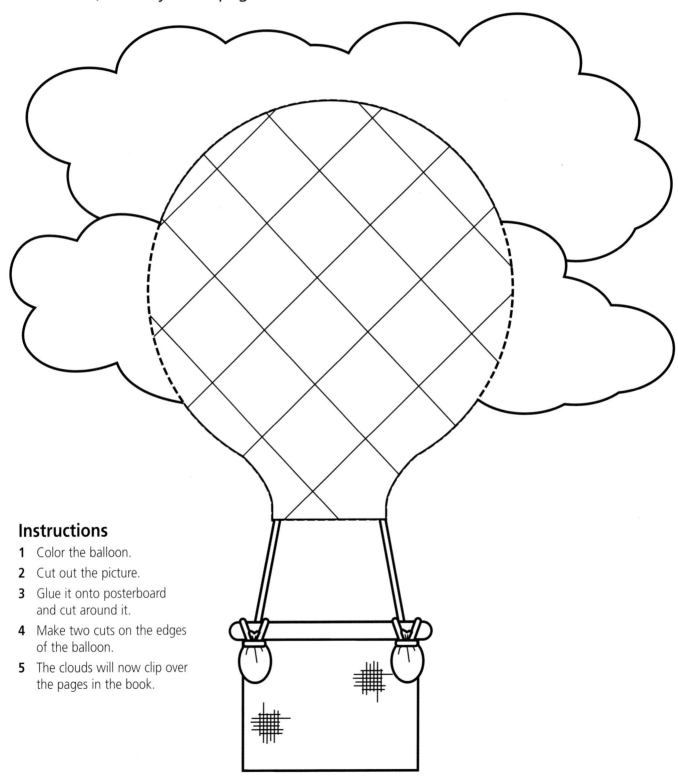

Instructions

1 Color the balloon.
2 Cut out the picture.
3 Glue it onto posterboard and cut around it.
4 Make two cuts on the edges of the balloon.
5 The clouds will now clip over the pages in the book.

Binoculars

Cut-out 2, Student's Book page 9

Instructions
1 Color the binoculars.
2 Cut them out.
3 Glue it onto posterboard, if possible.
4 Cut out the lenses.

Use the binoculars as shown on page 9 of the Student's Book.

© Cambridge University Press 2004   PHOTOCOPIABLE   Cut-out 2

Spinner

Cut-out 3, Activity Book page 9

Instructions
1 Color the spinner.
2 Cut it out.
3 Glue it onto posterboard and cut around it.
4 Push a pencil through the middle of the spinner.
5 Spin it!

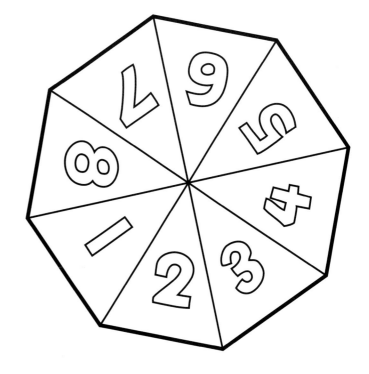

© Cambridge University Press 2004   PHOTOCOPIABLE   Cut-out 3

Spaceship

Cut-out 4, Student's Book page 17

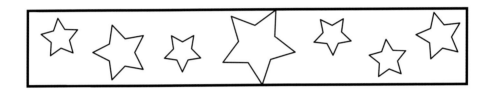

Instructions

See photographs in the Student's Book.
1. Color the strips (photo 1).
2. Cut them out (photo 2).
3. Curve them into a ring and tape the ends together (photo 3).
4. Tape each end of the straw inside one of the rings (photo 4).
5. Throw it!

Elephant trumpet

Cut-out 5, Student's Book page 35

Instructions

See photographs in the Student's Book.

1. Color the elephant's face and trunk strip (photo 1).
2. Cut out the two pieces (photo 2).
3. Cut out the hole for the mouth (photo 3).
4. Make folds as shown in photo 4. You can test the trumpet now. Hold it to your mouth and blow between the folds.
5. Make a tube from the trunk strip and glue it together down the side (photo 4). You can do this more easily if you wrap it around a pencil.
6. Attach the trunk to the face where the mouth is. Be carfeful not to block the hole in the face where the sound comes out.

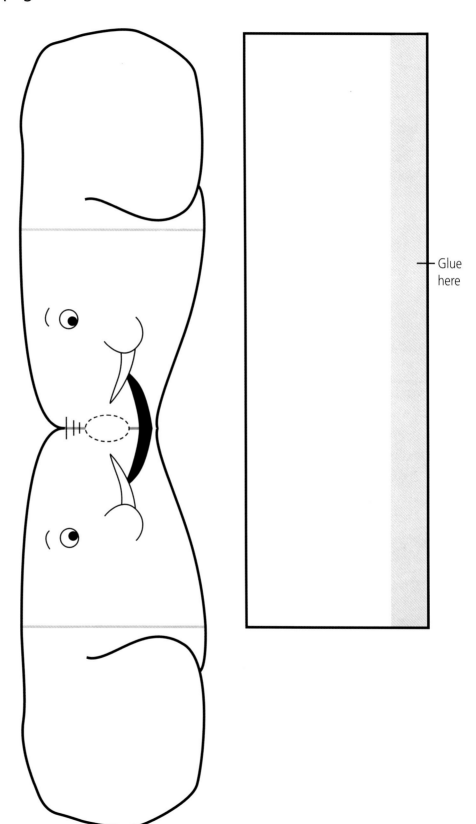

Glue here

© Cambridge University Press 2004   PHOTOCOPIABLE   Cut-out 5

T121

Strange animals

Cut-out 6, Student's Book page 38

Shark snapper

Cut-out 8, Student's Book page 53

Instructions

See photographs in the Student's Book.

1 Color the shark snapper and the fish (photo 1).
2 Glue them onto posterboard (photo 2).
3 Cut them out (photo 3).
4 Fold the shark in half.
5 Use tape to attach a piece of string inside the shark's mouth. Attach the other end of the string to the back of the fish (photo 4).
6 Let the fish hang down. With a jerking action, try to catch the fish in the shark's mouth.

Parrot

Cut-out 9, Student's Book page 61

Instructions

See photographs in the Student's Book.

1. Color the parrot.
2. Glue it onto posterboard.
3. Cut it out.
4. Try to balance the parrot on your finger. It will fall forward. Attach paper clips to the end of the tail as a counterweight, until the parrot balances on your finger.
5. You can balance the parrot on the back of your chair, on a pencil, or on the edge of a thin book.

Balloon mobile

Cut-out 10, Activity Book page 64

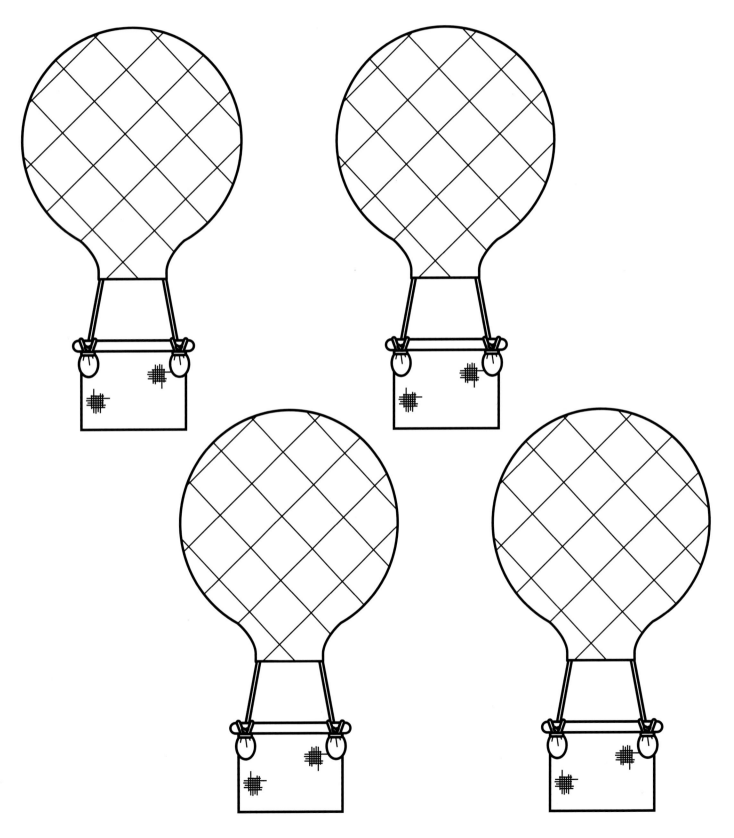

Acknowledgments

The authors and publishers are grateful to the following:
Editorial work by Cambridge University Press, Singapore.

Illustrations by Lizzie Finlay, c/o Heather Richards Agency; Susan Hutchison; Sue King, c/o SGA; David Shenton; Lisa Smith, c/o Sylvie Poggio Artists.

Photographic sources: Ardea pp. T97 *t*, T97 *br*; Bruce Coleman Collection pp. T97 *m,b*, T99 *bl*.

Commissioned photos by Gareth Boden Photography.

Book design and page make-up by Pentacor Book Design.

Cover design by Pentacor Book Design.

Cover illustration by David Shenton.

Freelance editorial work by Meredith Levy.
Freelance Americanization by Sabina Sahni-Davison.

Tests written by Meredith Levy.

Audio production by Rich LePage, LePage & Associates, New York.

Song words By Diana Hicks and Andrew Littlejohn.
Music by Robert Lee and Tim Wharton.